Poetry Pudding

By Christine Burrows

Front cover:
"Dolly's Poetry Pudding"
painted by Christine Burrows

Illustrations by Christine Burrows
unless otherwise stated.

All characters and events in this publication,
other than those clearly in the public domain,
are fictitious and any resemblance to real persons,
living or dead, is purely coincidental.

All Rights Reserved.
ISBN-9781709369896
MMXIX

Delicately Flawed

How delicately flawed are we,
we are uniquely scarred;
our imperfections there to see,
as all of us are marred.

And if we strive to be our best,
we trip and all fall down;
no one is better than the rest,
each one of us can drown.

Our journey has a winding road,
so free yourself of guilt;
the burden of a heavy load
can weigh us down when spilt.

Defenceless hearts are prone to break,
we none of us are free;
we all feel shame and make mistakes,
we're all the same you see.

Dedication

I dedicate this book to:
To my fellow Poets on Fanstory.com

Author's Preface:

This book includes over 270 poems written within the last eighteen months from 2017 to 2019 as the author has been actively posting two poems on line per day during this period. Poems written in many different formats including: Sonnet, Minute, Refrain, Villanelle, Rondeau, Rondeau Redouble, Nonet, Terza Rima, Blood Quill, Limerick, Kyrielle, Amphion, Sevenelle, Swap Quatrain, Pantoum, Tanka, Haiku, Acrostic, Petrarchan Sonnet, Loop, and Awdl Gynt, and even Rap! Also introducing the Awdl Sonnet and the Chime Operandi, both the author's own inventions.

This is a collection of short rhyming poems on a variety of subjects. Some will make you laugh, cry and soothe your soul. A mix of poems to suit your every mood that may amuse, take you to brave new worlds, or even rock your foundations. Poems from the heart, filled with emotion or historical facts that chill us to the core. Whichever poem you choose, you will be moved.

Expressing oneself in poetry releases feelings that are not often expressed in everyday life. We keep our emotions hidden inside us and the reader may realise they are not alone in their moment of need, these feelings are shared by us all.

Poetry for me leaves its mark on our lives. We all leave our footprint behind no matter how insignificant we think it is, we are all making history in our own back yard.

In all cultures, emotions are universally recognised, no matter who we are, we all have the same basic feelings. We are individuals with opinions. To be human is to err. We make a difference, even when we stumble. Delight in the pudding of life.

Enjoy: "Dolly's Poetry Pudding"

"Christine Burrows"

CONTENTS

A Beautiful Summer 1
A Blatant Bouquet 2
A Change will Come. 3
A Constant Groan. 4
A Fateful Journey. 5
A Fickle Heart. 6
A Happy Year 7
A Helping Hand 8
A Limerick 9
A Love Like That 10
A Perfumed Heart. 11
A Plane Ticket. 12/13
A Shadow Cast. 14
A Special Moment. 15
A Tearful Downfall 16
A Valued friend. 17
A Whisper 18
Accusations 19
Aerial Navigation System 20
Alcoholism 21
An English Summer. 22
An Ode to the Gardener. 23
An Ode to the Rose. 24
Another Child. 25
Appreciation. 26
Autumn and Winter 27
Ballooning in October. 28
Bare Wick. 29
Beach Toil 30
Before We Go. 31
Believe. 32
Big Boys, Noisy Toys 33
Big Titties. 34
Blinded by the Ruse. 35
Boo! 36
Boris, the Buffoon 37
Brenda on a Bender. 38
Captured Soul 39

iv

Cathedral Magnificence	40
Cause a Commotion	41
Chernobyl	42
Child Abuse	43
Christmas and New Year Memories	44
Christmas Thoughts	45
Cling to Sunny Afternoons	46
Coal Mining	47
Contentment	48
Continual Cascade	49
Controlling behaviour	50
Controlling Husbands	51
Corset Control	52
Cupid's Poor Aim	53
Dairy Milk	54
Day Break	55
Daylight Robbery	56
Deal, or no Deal	57
Dearest Mother	58
Death Row	59
Delightful Promises	60
Dirty Bertie	61
Dolly's Poetry Sweet Shop	62
Don't Leave Me	63
Double Standards	64
Dreams Come True	65
Drowning Sorrow	66
Deserving Rhyme	67
Empty	68
England, a Country Divided	69
Evening Glow	70
Facing Mortality	71
Fateful Path	72
Fear	73
Fern Made Firm	74
Flaws	75
Fly Away	76
Flying South	77
Forgive our Indiscretions	78

Forgive Yourself 79
Fractured Leadership. 80
Free as a Bird 81
Fresh Cream Cakes. 82
Friendships and Support. 83
Fun at the Fair. 84
Gender Swap. 85
Good Health. 86
Good Timing 87
Goodbye Grey Skies. 88
Goodbye Mrs May 89
Goosing Around 90
Gossip Girl. 91
Green Apple Pie 92
Halloween Tricksters. 93
Heads Up. 94
Heatwave 95
Her Star Eclipsed 96
Hesitation 97
Highwaymen. 98
Hope. 99
How Strange is Age. 100
I Caused a Stink 101
I Forgive the Past 102
Ilya Kuryakin. 103
I'm Missing You. 104
Immortality 105
In Treasured Chests 106
Insomniac. 107
Is There a God 108
It's Daybreak 109
Karate Chop. 110
King of Crime. 111
Knife Crime 112
Laws can Thwart Happiness. 113
Learning from Experience 114
Learning from Love. 115
Let Rip. 116
Live in Happiness 117

Long Summer Days	118
Lost to us	119
Love Across the Miles	120
Love Matters	121
Love Saved my Tears	122
Magical Moon Mapping	123
Man Up	124/125
Margherita Pizza	126
Marilyn	127
Mariposa Wings	128
Martyrs of the 17th Century	129
Mary Lost Her head	130
Meet the Geriatrics	131
Mental Illness	132
Memoirs	133
Memories	134
Memories inside my Heart	135
Merry Christmas and a Peaceful New Year	136
Misguided Rain	137
Missing Kissing	138
Mixing Colours	139
Mob Culture	140
Monarch of the Glen	141
Moon Phases	142
Mocking Lies	143
My Car and Me	144
My Insomnia	145
My New philosophy in Life	146
My Prince, my Knight	147
My Velvet Treasure Troves	148
Natures Sounds	149
Naughty Ghosts in Purgatory	150
No Switches	151
Noisy Days	152
Not So Funny	153
Nothing Changes	154
Oh Brenda	155
On Christmas Day	156
On England's Shores	157

On Foreign Soil.	158
Open Hearts.	159
Orgasmic.	160
Over Sexed and Over Here.	161
Painful Memories.	162
Past Loving Times.	163
Peace.	164
Perfect Christmas Chimes.	165
Perfect Roses.	166
Perfumed Attraction.	167
Perky Poetry.	168
Pivoting Petals.	169
Please Help?.	170
Poor Granny.	171
Quentin, I love You!.	172
Rainy June.	173
Rectified Dysfunction.	174
Revenge is Sweet.	175
RIP on the Streets.	176/177
Ruth.	178
Sad News.	179
Salute Red Admiral.	180
Santa Indulges.	181
Santa Likes a Curry.	182
School Days.	183
Seasoned reality.	184
Second Hand Rose.	185
Serengeti.	186
Shadows.	187
Shot for Love.	188
Sleep Deprived.	189
Smelling the Roses.	190
Smooth as Butter.	191
Snow and Ice.	192
Some will Hang.	193
Storms.	194
Strawberry Tarts.	195
Stubborn.	196
Stink Like a Skunk.	197

Summer Scenes	198
Sunny Roses	199
Sweet Dandelions (The Happy Weed)	200
Sweet Valentine	201
Take a Walk with Nature	202
Take Care	203
Tell the Truth	204
Tempestuousness	205
Temptation	206
That Fateful Day	207
The Battle Scars	208/209
The Big Guys Always Win	210
The Botticelli Bather	211
The Britishers	212
The Chime Operandi	213
The Cleaners	214
The Cockroach Education Seminar	215
The Cycle of Life	216
The Dance of the Ostrich	217
The Dangerous Past	218
The Dawn Chorus	219
The Drug Dealer	220
The Earth, Moon and Sun	221
The Fateful Flanders Fields	222
The Field of War	223
The food Chain	224
The Get Away	225
The Hospital Doom	226
The Irish Question	227
The Lichfield Bower	228
The Lovers Brew	229
The Marriage Bond	230
The Moon Remembers	231
The Old Soldier	232
The Perfect Feminist	233
The Power of Money	234
The Power of Poetry	235
The Prowling Vampire	236
The Rise of the Nazis	237

The Rook.	238
The Salon.	239
The Search is on.	240
The Seasons.	241
The Secret Poet.	242
The Sparkle Returns	243
The Storm would Spread.	244
The Things we Used to Do.	245
The Truth Hurts.	246
The Vapour Dragons.	247
There is a Cost.	248
These Angel Wings.	249
They Took Old Dolly Down	250
This Child of Mine.	251
Three's a Crowd.	252
Tick Tock.	253
Time has Grace.	254
Time Reflecting.	255
To friendships.	256
To Pick a Flower.	257
Trees Grow Leaves.	258
Troubling Critics.	259
Turn the Page of Age	260
Uncle Scrooge.	261
Unfaithful.	262
Winsome Butterfly Wings.	263
Waking up my Muse.	264
Walking into Disaster.	265
We Thank You Ma'am.	266
Welcome to the back Stabbers.	267
Well Endowed.	268
What Lies Beneath.	269
What Pigeons Like.	270
Winter Struggles.	271
Wishing on a Star.	272
Witch Hunt.	273
You are not Alone.	274
Author's Biography.	275
Dolly's Poetry Pudding.	276

A Beautiful Summer

When spring blooms with a pretty daffodil,
my heart then has the will to watch the show;
how still are trees, but soon leaves have the skill,
to shoot from darkened branches under snow.

And once the green has taken hold once more,
then nothing stops the store of wealth beneath.
Exploring early light, the birds at four,
bring song they've finely tuned into a tweet,

as June and July warm the parks with sun,
my roses have begun to bring their joy,
the fun of summer has a good long run
to share with every girl and every boy.

The lazy days are in my memory,
I view them when it's only snow I see.

A Blatant Bouquet

The perfumed bottle I know well,
a shell, with life inside.
The scent denied because the smell,
reminded me I cried.
The day I wore this pretty spray,
a prayer was said
a mournful shed
of tears I dread,
my life it's said,
is dead within this sad bouquet.

A Change Will Come

When winter breezes bring unwelcome chills,
remember spring is waiting to create
a change is guaranteed upon those hills.

Though life can be a trial when trouble spills,
the icy hand of hate will not abate,
when winter breezes bring unwelcome chills.

A shadow falls and many turn to pills,
to bear the burden of the heavy weight,
a change is guaranteed upon those hills.

As nothing is so bad, unless it kills,
another day surprisingly can wait,
when winter breezes bring unwelcome chills.

As new buds yearn to colour with their frills,
there's hope for us to steer a better fate,
a change is guaranteed upon those hills.

Sweet scented flowers patiently use skills,
despite the snow they bud for nature's sake,
when winter breezes bring unwelcome chills,
a change is guaranteed upon those hills.

A Constant Groan

Why do we hear a constant groan,
that life is this and that?
Our tongues bore through our very soul,
we hate our habitat.

We can't accept a day that's wet,
for we think it will last;
but flowers quench their dry pipettes
they drink so very fast.

And if someone offended us,
and thus, dissolved our heart,
a word not meant to cause a fuss,
said by someone not smart.

Remember that a ray of sun
is warm upon our head,
be glad a new day has begun,
for soon we'll all be dead.

A Fateful Journey

I believed in a word
when it jumped from the page
as the truth had a deadly attack.
As the news in my world
bubbled up in a rage
and my life was thrown onto its back.

As the future was bleak,
and my eye now so blind,
as the road ahead twisted and damned.
On this path I would seek
to find some peace of mind,
and accept all the fate that was planned.

A Fickle Heart

What we have shared is fickle like the wind,
without those firming roots, there is no tree;
and when the candle light is slowly dimmed,

my heart is yours and under lock and key.
Yet I will spend so many hours alone,
divided is your time and loyalty,

my soul is weighted down by heavy stone,
if only love would glow without such pride,
relieve the aching grief that bares my bone.

Alas I dare not speak the truth inside,
for fear your heart will run, and not confide.

A Happy Year

A happy year for everyone
this new year almost has begun.
As twenty thousand and nineteen,
will be the best year we have seen
as fun and joy's bestowed upon . . .

the moon and stars, also the sun
will brighten heart's so we become
encouraged, happy and will mean
a happy year.

As joys are sometimes overdone
bring tears of memories that stun
and Auld Lang Syne, our cheerful theme
we'll sing with friends as tears will stream
be grateful for the days to come . . .
a happy year.

A Helping Hand

I know not of his gracious face,
his wealth or status in the race;
or of his robes of golden thread,
or where he rests his weary head.
A stranger here gave help in need,
his heart of gold
shone very bold,
he rescued me,
that's all I see,
an angel sent to do a deed.

I didn't ask from whence he came,
or question if he knew my name,
or what religion he swore within,
the shade of skin he was born in,
or whether he liked this or that,
he gave me all,
he saw me fall,
humanity
gave gravity
to this man's soul, and that's a fact.

A Limerick

When writing with words, I believe,
that a Limerick I might conceive.
I start with a grin,
as rhythms kick in,
and the magic of rhyme intervenes.

A Love Like That

I'm looking for a love like that,
a love that lasts and knows
that if I'm old and gaining fat,
it's still me that love chose.

I'm looking for a love like that,
the kind and caring sort,
not independent like a cat,
a love that can't be bought.

I'm looking for a love like that
I've seen on silver screens
to feel inside a big impact,
an inner light that beams.

I'm looking for a love like that
I knew when I was young,
that love that puts the flutter back,
when love was newly sprung.

"Dolly's Poetry Pudding"

A Perfumed Heart

Her beauty turns so many heads,
this pretty rose
with perfect pose
has love inside that spreads and spreads.

In ignorance
this innocence

in petalled leaves so soft and pure
will soothe your soul
and make it whole,
her perfumed heart has just the cure.

A Plane Ticket

A printed ticket in my hand
the queue too long from where I stand
and finally I'm at the gate
I am then told that I must wait.

I feel that I have been coerced,
for those who paid, are boarding first.
No plane is on the tarmac yet,
but we are herded, neck by neck.

Our bodies stuffed into a funnel,
suspended high, this stilted tunnel.
So many very grumpy men
are hanging high inside this pen.

The crew in uniforms demand
that we must all obey commands;
no time to offer helping hands,
we need to go, so we can land!

I wave my wife off to the right
she's in front, I'm out of sight.
exhausted I now take my seat
It's been so long, I feel dead beat.

The dolly trolley has no tea
my seat is at the end you see,
hot snacks are sold, no food to eat
I'm strapped for hours in this seat.

"Dolly's Poetry Pudding"

Reclining is forbidden dear,
my legs too long for this space here,
The queueing and the lack of food
means I arrive in blackened mood.

A trumpet sounding in my ear
as Ryanair announce with cheer!
An 'on-time' flight is their big boast
expecting to propose a toast.

Do customers have any clout?
We're herded like dumb sheep .. about.
When paying for a single seat
my holiday seems incomplete.

And Ryanair should take good heed
give us a hostess of good breed,
a smile to greet with pretty face
not moaning staff who hate our case.

Be courteous and caring too,
help that old man get to the loo,
give us a seat, at lower cost,
should never mean we suffer loss.

A Shadow Cast

When Christmas seemed a long way off
please do not scoff
or groan and moan
how time has flown!

This season's celebration here
is full of cheer . . .
but not for those
without a rose.

Remember those who live alone,
remain unknown,
live in the past,
a shadow cast.

A Special Moment

When living every moment,
I see life slipping by,
the sun can move extremely fast
when it begins to die.

And as the darkness kills the light
another day has gone;
and sleep will close my eyes too soon,
before my writing's done.

And words will taunt my dreams each night
they form in complex lines,
and when the blackbird wakes to light,
I hear him sing in rhymes.

Reminding me to listen hard,
let his song fill my heart,
these special minutes held within,
until he then departs.

A Tearful Downpour

Why is it that this clouded shroud,
forecasts the thunder very loud?
The shower pours and wet I get,
and every raindrop, won't forget.

You said goodbye and now I cry,
and I can't mend this tearful sky,
no sun will shine, I'm in decline.
Why did you break this heart of mine?

A Valued Friend

I learned to know the value of a friend,
someone to trust when all the chips are down,
as some were born to give and some pretend.

The winding road of life comes to an end,
we harvest crops and never let them drown,
I learned to know the value of a friend.

Our choices mean we may have to defend,
supporting will be where our love is found,
as some were born to give and some pretend.

A mutual respect will then depend,
on building good foundations from the ground,
I learned to know the value of a friend.

A friend will never patronise or send
a word of false betrayal to confound,
as some were born to give and some pretend.

And if you find a diamond, I commend
you treasure every moment they're around,
I learned to know the value of a friend,
as some were born to give and some pretend.

A Whisper

The whisper fled into the air
and wasn't meant to share out there.
The rumour started.
It spread as it was flaming hot
a bolt of hate from bow was shot
it was cold hearted.

And pistols drawn were held in hands
revenge was never even planned,
as hurtful spite was put about,
the whisper didn't have to shout.

A rift between two friends had grown,
because the whisper was well known.
Deceitful was this cruel attack,
as words cannot be taken back.

Accusations

When mud is thrown it sticks like glue,
as words resound,
become profound,
try shaking them when they're untrue.

Embed in you,
like ink tattoo.

The dirty words that people throw
begin to moan,
a seed is sown
and doubt will grow, deep down below.

"Christine Burrows"

Aerial Navigation System

There once was a fat pigeon from Rome,
who could not navigate his way home,
he pooped all the way,
bright white on display,
and the moon lit his own aerodrome.

Illustration by: Isabella Maya Shepherd

ALCOHOLISM

Anaesthetised by gin at dawn
I'm guaranteed
a liquid feed
before reality is born.

A drunken state
is my best mate.

Addicted to this thing I crave,
another shot
will hit the spot,
and take me to an early grave.

AN ENGLISH SUMMER

My memory becomes unclear
each precious year in June.
I try to make the view appear,
when gazing at the moon.
     Alas it's been so many months
     again I try without results,
     if only I could see just once,
an English afternoon.

I yearn to hear the choir sing,
at home where my heart lies,
and when the crocus says: 'it's spring,'
I'll journey through the skies
     to see the robin red and bright,
     the dandelion seed take flight,
     the willow tree dance with delight,
such scenes enchant my eyes.

I won't forget the smiles of those,
who give me all their love.
The fresh smell of an English rose,
the rainfall from above.
     The baking of the sour dough bread.
     The long sleep in my king sized bed.
     Words said in English in my head.
The cooing of a dove.

And when I hear cathedral bells,
they're chiming every hour
The yellow jasmine's fragrant smells
are blooming on the bower,
     I'll know I'll be back home again,
     to feel the sun and drops of rain,
     familiar is this wet terrain,
I see the spring in flower.

AN Ode to the Gardener

The local men are hoeing every bed
as parks await the splendid colour spread;
and trees, like ancient pillars, looking on,
will witness petals open to the sun.
As rustling leaves applauding has begun,
the hand of man will rear a pretty bloom
to plant in rows to cheer the dreary gloom.

The rain will fall and quench the earth's rich soil,
and bees will swear allegiance to their toil.
The birds in chorus compliment the scene,
their music helps alleviate routine.
And marigolds add hints of tangerine,
the hand of man will rear a pretty bloom
to plant in rows to cheer the dreary gloom.

"Christine Burrows"

An Ode to the Rose

A rose knows she is beautiful,
she does not know she fades;
she blooms and pleases with her scent
does not repent her shades.

Her petals tinged with rusty hues,
her heart still shines within,
and she believes in good reviews
refusing to give in.

The dying rose remembers well
her debut perfectly,
and as she dies she promises
so unreservedly . . .

to bloom again with great delight,
reliably on time.
The rose will serve us time again,
and some may even climb.

Another Child

If I could live my time again,
I'd change this one small thing.
Another child I would have had
their song would make me sing.

Decisions ruled by finances
kept our kids to two.
If only I had fought for three
I would have then met you.

But pressures of our hectic life,
with work as busy bees,
no time to have another child,
so it was not conceived.

When I look back, the choice was wrong,
we should have had another
and added to the family fun
a sister or a brother.

But this regret has futile roots
the past is set in stone.
I'll concentrate on just my two,
be happy and atone.

My two now have two kids each,
four little ones are here,
I can't believe I had such luck,
not two, but six now cheer!

Appreciation

Now give yourself a minute here
a little cheer
inside your heart
before you start.

A moment to take stock of things,
a birdie sings,
a flowering shrub,
or little grub.

A second just to hear the sound
to touch the ground,
and smell the earth,
and know your worth.

Before the grind of day begins,
with hectic spins.
Slow minutes down,
so you don't drown.

Autumn and Winter

The golden shroud looms overhead,
as breezes cool us down,
the colour fades to brown, now dead,
when autumn starts to crown.

The footpath softened under foot,
with slippy wet brown leaves,
it's time to leave the shrinking wood
before the winter freeze.

As preparations soon become
a sign that ice will form;
the bitter cold, without the sun,
and soon there'll be a storm.

The azure sky will turn to grey,
the robin will appear
against a blanket white display
the scene will be austere.

My fear of winter you have guessed
is very real for me;
the long cold days I do protest,
of crisp intensity.

So I will bid the land farewell
escape to warmer parts,
and find another place to dwell,
though saddened are some hearts.

Ballooning in October

The crisp October morning came
I wore my scarf and gloves,
I saw balloons heat with a flame
today I'll fly with doves.

The ship, so big and colourful
I climbed aboard to fly,
I thought how simply wonderful
to reach and touch the sky.

And as I soared across the fields
of gold and auburn brown
the changing season now reveals,
a flaxen tree lined crown.

The people waved as I passed by
and I could feel the breeze,
I did not rock, destabilise,
I did not even sneeze!

Illustration by Indira Kimberley Shepherd

Bare Wick

There was an old man who liked posing
in parks where old ladies were dozing
onlookers were sick
when he bared his wick
reporting the man for exposing!

Beach Toil

The tired beach now wants to rest
the flowing tide
cleans far and wide
and smooths the footprints in its quest.

as setting sun
means day is done.

Tomorrow shores begin their chores,
the toiling sand
withstands demand;
the beach confronts the saboteurs.

Before We Go!

The ticking clock will run amok,
in history our time is locked.
Mortality put on a block,
will run amok, the ticking clock.

As time runs out, we start to shout,
to chart our years we are devout;
and memories we laugh about,
we start to shout, as time runs out.

Before we go, enjoy the show,
there's so much more for us to know,
soon buried are we down below
enjoy the show, before we go!

BeLieVe

Dreams
when they are denied . . .
put your faith in tomorrow

Big Boys, Noisy Toys

How boys just love to make a noise,
with hammers, nails and drilling toys,
they care not what the neighbours think,
and many heads in hands will sink,
the sound of engines loud and clear;
like grinding wheels
of steel to steel;
the cranking clang
and bumping bang,
instils a kind of dreadful fear.

This manmade noise, a curse to earth,
is this our legacy, our worth?
When nature's music is downed out,
with dreadful pounding all about;
oh please let silence soon descend;
then ears will flirt
with rustling skirt
of willow sway,
a breeze at play,
on these sweet sounds we can depend.

Big Titties

There once was a girl with big titties
who tired of men's sexual quickies;
she wanted it slow,
to reach a plateau,
all men had this stubborn Achilles.

BLiNded by tHe RuSe

If I could see beyond the veil
and not be blinded using Braille,
I'd know the truth behind the scene,
be sure if someone's really mean,
my x-ray eye would never fail.

I'd see the fall before the wail,
protect the weak, and help the frail.
Inform you all, I would be keen,
if I could see.

As some will hide the small detail,
until completed is the sale,
when it's too late to intervene,
the fraud becomes something obscene.
I should have listened to this tale,
if I could see.

"Christine Burrows"

Boo!

Ghosts are on the loose
the element of surprise
hangs on fear itself

Boris, the Buffoon

Oh Boris what are you to do,
now that your hopeful dream came true?
To be the PM was your goal,
the job may even steal your soul!

A monkey or a keen buffoon,
could play the role, and end it soon,
for Europe will not deal with us,
because we have made such a fuss;

and you will stomp around with fame,
so selfishly you'll make a name,
the biggest fool we ever had,
as your persona makes us mad.

As you compare yourself to men,
like Churchill, time and time again,
we are not blind, as we're inclined
to think that you have lost your mind!

A look-a-like to Mr Trump,
we want to see how high you jump?
And like a ball you will bounce back
no matter who tries to attack.

Your skin is thick and brains are thin,
we know your life is steeped in sin,
can you save us from certain hell?
We're on the edge, and time will tell.

Brenda on a Bender

There once was a woman named Brenda,
who loved getting drunk on a bender,
one night she met Steve,
who planned to deceive,
for he had a diff'rent agenda!

Captured Soul

Venus flytrap
awaits innocent unarmed wings
cruel soulless death threat

"Christine Burrows"

Cathedral Magnificence

Cathedral
the peaceful steeple spires
chiming sounds that call me to her heart.

Open doors
enticing treasure chest
historic magnificence within.

Powerful,
a decorative façade,
and un-obstructive view . . . seen for miles.

Lichfield Cathedral

Cause a Commotion

To rhyme your lines and make them chime
with assonance and cheer,
remember poems need to reach
the reader's inner ear;
not just words that sound the same,
but words that tear apart,
evoke emotion, rock the ocean
deep inside their heart.

Chernobyl

This horror stares me in the face
and leaves a dreadful bitter trace,
contamination left to spread
and killing us when in our bed.
The particles are cancerous,
but no one shouted, made a fuss.
The party rules the roost out here
and everybody lives in fear.

The Graphite looks like blackened coal,
but if you touch this acid mould,
fire will burn you outside in
and inside it will kill within.
The air we breathe is thick and black
an atmosphere that will attack.
For miles around this impure air
has left an evil that we share.

A graveyard that is metal clad,
is concrete-filled, and this is bad,
impurity is grinding deep
through earth and stone it likes to creep.
This power mankind has invented,
was left to fester, then fermented.
The bodies melting look absurd,
and grieving sobs can still be heard.

Child Abuse

The inner sanctum is revealed,
an evil seed has been unsealed.
as poetry's concerned with truth,
to speak of wounds left there by youth.

And time can never ease the pain,
aggrieved beneath by hidden rain,
and visits to the past unseen,
reveal the dirty deed unclean.

Between the sheets where privately
a crime committed sexually,
has left a gaping scar of woe,
that no one ever came to know.

For those around with blinkered eyes,
did not hear cries of secret lies.

Christmas and New Year Memories

Oh Christmas Eve when Santa calls,
we deck the halls,
and in the snow;
his coat will glow.

Oh Christmas Day, please shine for me,
the twinkling tree
so colourful,
a magic pull.

Oh New Year's day let us be bright,
we saw last night,
the sparkling skies
as last year dies.

Christmas Thoughts

As Christmas day's not far away
and this I say,
let turkeys live
they will forgive.

Now hang your stocking on the tree,
not all are free
those on the streets
will get no treats.

I pray that Santa makes your day,
and fights his way
to your abode
to leave his load.

Cling to Sunny Afternoons

When you are being blamed for everything,
your heart is racing and you feel a fool,
remember not to cling to words that sting.

Not every flower blooms when it is spring,
sometimes the weather's cold and it is cruel,
when you are being blamed for everything.

It may be hard for some to hear you sing
and some are blinded by your special jewel,
remember not to cling to words that sting.

Now wounded, you will need to mend your wing
and learn from nature's ever changing rule,
when you are being blamed for everything.

As long as happy hearts with love still bring
the sun into your summer afternoon,
remember not to cling to words that sting.

When jealousy can throw mud at a King,
then always keep your head and keep your cool,
when you are being blamed for everything,
remember not to cling to words that sting.

Coal Mining

In a blink of an eye, his whole life had become
such a drudge, as the pit, ruled the roost;
early morn, every day, down a hole, he'd be gone,
on his skin, only black was produced.

In his hair, under nails, as the coal penetrates,
and he scrubbed really hard to be clean;
but the coal was a curse, as it still decorates
dirty skin where the coal has been keen.

Under ground is a life that is not very good
and the men risk their lives every day;
as they all could be dead if the pit's not secured,
and the men lose their lives in this way.

CONTENTMENT

My observation tells me that in youth,
we constantly are looking for the truth.
Our fight may take us into the affray,
and rarely do we look the other way.

We search with keen wide eyes for such a place,
where perfectly we fit and can embrace;
and when the rain floods thoughts inside our head,
the misty view may cloud the course we tread.

With hindsight we look back on foolish times,
we failed to read the glaring warning signs,
now wiser, we have learned to fill our cup,
as day to day sweet pleasures are enough.

Contentment is well earned, I have been told,
and peaceful afternoons are worth pure gold,
a smile can lift the spirit deep inside,
and gone is all our angst and foolish pride.

Continual Cascade

One drop of rain on this terrain,
in a continual cascade.
Grey clouds became a dreary pain,
meticulous on this parade.

In a continual cascade,
the pitter patter does not end.
Meticulous on this parade
on rainfall trees and plants depend.

The pitter patter does not end,
it swamps the paths, blocks up the drain,
on rainfall trees and plants depend,
on drops of rain on this terrain.

It swamps the paths, blocks up the drain,
the heavy pour will never stop;
with drops of rain on this terrain,
I hear it constantly go plop.

The heavy pour will never stop,
in thundering an escapade;
I hear the constant plop, plop plop!
I see green fields the rain has made.

In a continual cascade,
we thank the heavens for the rain,
to keep the fields greenly displayed,
more drops required for this terrain.

Controlling Behaviour

Look! There goes that man, with his down trodden wife,
controlled all her movements, for most of her life;
and she cannot function without his say so,
she never sees places, she would like to go;

and she is a shadow of her former self,
no freedom to work, or accumulate wealth;
a lifetime of 'do's', and the 'don'ts' she has heard,
but she has accepted, his every word.

Her eyes are devoid, of a sparkle somehow,
resigned to a life with some bitterness now;
and she serves her purpose, and this women knows,
that he was the man that she faithfully chose.

Twas not his intention to drive her away,
but he made pretty sure, that she would not stray;
and his heavy hand took its toll on her soul,
as without him to share, she wouldn't feel whole.

This saddened behaviour is often the case,
as man's insecurities often debase;
but he is the loser, her heart was denied
he took all her joy, and her great sense of pride.

Controlling Husbands

He never said they would be friends,
concerns can often smother,
and loyalty in love extends,
to then include the Mother.

As jealousy grew deep in veins,
to share her would not do.
A silent word can often pain,
her daughter then withdrew.

And letting go is oh so hard,
when flesh and blood are one,
and time went by in this regard,
she felt that he had won.

But chinks appeared along the way,
control can wear quite thin,
by stepping out she had no say,
her soul . . . destroyed within.

Her Mother knew she had no voice,
this girl had lost her heart,
although she had no other choice,
she loved him from the start.

And Mothers always will support
their daughters when in need,
but most of all they have been taught,
that life's best lived, when freed.

Corset Control

There was a young woman from Dorset,
who ate too much food for her corset;
her stays popped like corks,
when she went for walks,
steel girders should have reinforced it.

Cupid's Poor Aim

There was a mad man from the city,
who chased every girl who was pretty.
But he met his match,
when Cupid dispatched,
an arrow shot straight through his willy.

"Christine Burrows"

Dairy Milk

Guilty pleasures soothe . . .
like chocolate on the tongue,
a heavenly taste
momentarily fulfils
indulgent naughty cravings.

Daybreak

The darkness shifts, and highlights lift,
as daybreak soothes the night,
so very soon I see the gift
of morning sun delight.

With promises of brand new scenes,
new waves of life begin,
and on a cloud of hopeful dreams,
each day I hope to win.

As opportunity in life
is born when we awake,
as dawn will take away the strife,
new promises to make.

When the sun lifts up its head
and glistens on the sea,
I know it's time to leave my bed,
and celebrate with glee.

Daylight Robbery

Decisions made to tax my light
And dim all sunny days.
Yes blacked are windows into night,
Left me without a gaze.
Infused with thirst, the government,
Gave warning that we heed.
Have boarded windows with cement
To satisfy their greed.

Robbed of sincere morality,
Obfuscated daylight,
Brought stark dark cold reality
Because they stole my sight.
Enforced a law that we deplore
Reduced the public to the floor
Yes hindsight is contrite.

The window tax was introduced in England during the 18th and 19th Centuries. The tax was simply based on how may windows a house had. Windows everywhere were bricked up to avoid the tax.

In England you can see many ancient buildings with their windows bricked up to this day. A legacy of a stupid tax that dimmed the inside of many houses.

Deal, or No Deal

Oh Churchill! Where are you when needed most?
Our parliament has not fared well of late;
The future is a fearful phantom fate,
and haunting Britain like poor Marley's ghost.
The Deal . . . a narrow minded short riposte.
Division in the house in such a state,
the Europeans have closed their golden gate.
Your steely strong determination lost,

and weak are knees from such negotiation;
why did we tangle up a strengthened knot?
We need your expertise to free our nation.
Nostalgic folk who yearn for times forgot,
now need your wise and thoughtful inspiration,
before foundations crumble from this plot.

Dearest Mother

The Singer was all full of thread
she made a cotton skirt of red;
I wore it to the high school dance,
embroidered stitching had enhanced
the fabric that she bought in France.
T'was on that summer day in June
my dearest Mother left too soon.

The skirt of red with well sown seams,
was made with love and tender dreams;
my daughter wore it to a show
and gave the skirt a special glow,
as tears begin to overflow,
t'was on that summer day in June
my dearest Mother left too soon.

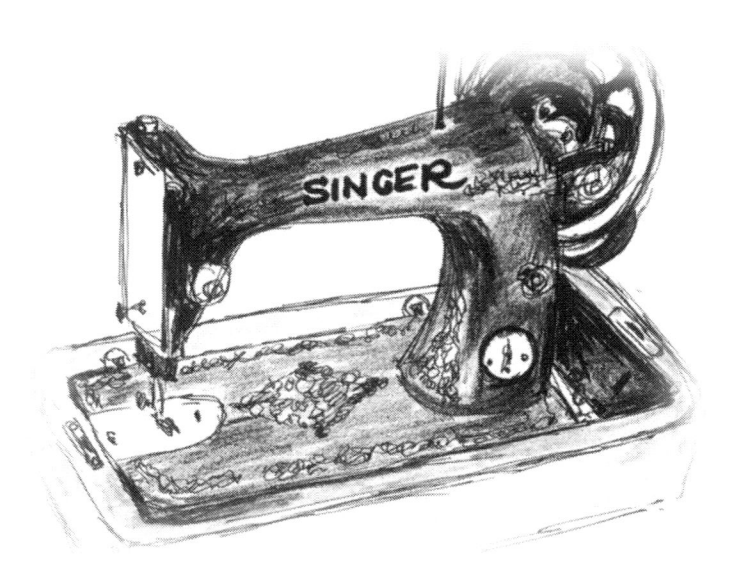

Death Row

When death is legalised by man, it's odd;
as killing breaks the basic rule of law:
tomorrow is not in the hands of God.

"And men live on 'the mile' inside a fog,
without the chance to see an open door,
when death is legalised by man, it's odd.

To put a man to sleep just like a dog,
and no one can admit there is a flaw,
tomorrow is not in the hands of God."

The double standards here leave me agog,
a lynching means to even up the score,
when death is legalised by man, it's odd.

An execution stay stagnates the bog,
the reaper and the law have good rapport,
tomorrow is not in the hands of God.

And every day death serves a toxic smog,
prolonging life to reach the final shore,
when death is legalised by man, it's odd,
tomorrow is not in the hands of God.

"Christine Burrows"

Delightful Promises

saffron daffodils
the Easter bonnet brigade
pledge to spring early

Dirty Bertie

There once was a vagrant from Turkey,
who slept on the streets and was dirty.
His pong was quite strong
when he washed his thong,
and all of the water turned murky.

Dolly's Poetry Sweet Shop

Dip inside this little book
Only for a minute.
Life can sometimes shake us up,
Lively is our spirit.
Yellow daffodils can please,
Sweet smells can change our mood,

Poetry can soothe and ease,
Orators can intrude.
Every word can move a heart,
Tantalise . . . console,
Read a phrase in here to start
Your journey to your soul.

Sow a seed inside your mind
Weather every storm;
Even if someone's unkind
Evaluate . . . reform.
To make a change, can be strange,

Shops provide the wares,
Hope and love and faith can change,
Open hearts with prayers.
Poetry will soothe inside, repair all your affairs.

Don't Leave Me

Don't leave me here, I need you dear,
without you I would shed a tear,
your presence is always sincere,
I need you dear, don't leave me here.

So stay with me, and let it be,
do not waste time, as life you see,
is better spent, when trouble-free,
so let it be, and stay with me.

Our time is short, we are then taught,
to never make ourselves distraught,
to keep our hearts from being fraught,
we are then taught, our time is short.

Double Standards

The army marched in unison
in regimented black;
for one of them, the day had come
to break free from the pack.

He saw his opportunity
deserted all the rest,
and hoping for immunity
of war he did protest.

He ran away to save his skin
as fear was in his veins;
as killing thwarted him within,
his conscience was in chains.

One day his secret was described,
was under close arrest.
His hands and feet securely tied,
there was no last request

At dawn a squad of stealthy men
loaded up their guns.
In unison they shot their friend,
he'd see no setting suns.

The moral of this chilling tale,
the law to kill can change;
morality is up for sale
when rules of war engage.

Dreams Can Come True

There was a man homeless from Walford,
one night met a rich man who sponsored;
to luck he held tight.
as his inner light,
shone bright on his talent, he prospered.

Drowning Sorrow

He's drowning sorrow late at night,
as with himself he had a fight,
and soon the scent of liquor quelled
the inner pain inside that dwelled.
He drank not one, but many more,
    that brought him sleep,
    from whisky neat,
    with no more cries
    he closed his eyes;
and in his dreams he could explore.

The day was late, he lay awake,
and prayed to God, his life He'd take,
a cigarette, began to smoke.
The empty cans and bottles there
reminded him of his despair.
He needed just a drop of gin
    to face the day,
    and in a sway,
    unsteady feet
    were in defeat,
he knew that he was dead within.

Deserving Rhyme

This rhyming verse just may appeal
with zeal it rhymes with pride.
it pops inside to make you feel,
that poetry can glide.
To sing with clever sounding words,
to feel the chime,
internal rhyme,
can be a sign
I'm in decline . . .
a crime to join poetic nerds.

Empty

How empty, empty is my glass,
it is no longer full;
he pulled away from this sweet girl,
my world now rather dull.

An empty bed, and empty life,
a hole appeared in me;
a void I can no longer fill,
he took away the key.

How blind I was, I did not see,
that helpless little boy,
who can't let go and set me free
and played me like a toy.

So real is life, that love can hurt,
those words exchanged so strong;
but I could never reach his heart
and what he did was wrong.

Now both alone to lick our wounds
no longer I look back;
a selfish view, just will not do,
as love's a two way track.

England, a country divided

Whilst there is breath within our lungs,
and life still burns with fire and pride,
fight on against those wagging tongues.

As angry thunder overcomes,
we'll counteract the raging tide,
whilst there is breath within our lungs,

In wars there may be sounding guns,
and sad regretful tears be cried,
fight on against those wagging tongues.

Despite the sounding of the drums,
let hearts lead on and be our guide,
whilst there is breath within our lungs.

To see our country's setting suns
fall on a once united stride,
fight on against those wagging tongues.

For England's hands are truly tied,
a resolution is denied,
whilst there is breath within our lungs,
fight on against those wagging tongues.

EVENING GLOW

Canarian sky
fire-beam in tangerine
splendent waves of dye

Facing Mortality

His blank stare spoke a thousand words,
he would not see tomorrow,
behind his eyes there were concerns,
and heavy was his sorrow.

For he would not be there to fight,
protect and care for those . . .
his family who saw his light
fade when his eyes were closed.

He died before his final breath,
he saw reality . . .
and face to face he would see death,
his own mortality.

Fateful Path

Our fate is in our character,
referring to our trait,
as we relate and sometimes stir,
as temper can dictate.
Decisions made then steer a course
to early graves,
as we are slaves
to fateful ways
as life decays
in ways that fill us with remorse.

Fear

When fear can thwart with what might then be true,
anticipation grew and grew inside,
as you and I will dread a future view,
because our fear stems from something implied.

A picture printed clearly, understood,
of sorrow that could bud from what we know,
that should not stop us in our tracks for good,
but we will let the fear consume and grow,

To our surprise our fear is so misguided,
we should not have confided in the lie,
providing fuel, now fear has all subsided,
as what we thought would happen passed us by.

The stresses and the strains of life today,
destroy our faith and give our soul away.

Fern Made Firm

There was once a young woman named Fern,
with a knack as a whore to make firm,
she lined up the men,
and counted to ten,
and she didn't know which way to turn.

FLaWS

Sometimes we're flawed in love and life,
experience is keen,
and in between the joy, there's strife,
we learn that life is mean.

Within the dirty water pond,
a lily thrives so bright;
and then we forge a loving bond,
that makes us want to fight!

And balancing the yin and yang
is troubling at times,
but then we see the roses hang,
from fences so divine.

So now we look and see the joy
the world brings to our eyes,
and never let someone annoy,
or hear their woeful cries.

If we can see the good out there,
the special scenes that please,
our hearts will have the love to share
to make flaws melt with ease.

Fly Away

I flew up in the sky today,
to northern shores with greener parks;
where cloudy skies will burst in May,
as showers drench, and leave their marks.

I see the sun and touch the stars,
I flew up in the sky today.
And thoughts of parks now heal my scars,
as rainbow skies are on display.

Where rooks and robins always play,
and pigeons rule in my home town.
I flew up in the sky today,
I'll soon be landing on the ground.

I see the landscape of new scenes,
as I am high and feel the sway,
a change from boring old routines,
I flew up in the sky today.

Flying South

My plane awaits, I take my seat
and leave behind the cloudy street,
these icy roads you need your skates
I take my seat, my plane awaits.

To sunny shores I'll fly today,
and leave you to the cloudy day,
as up into the sky it soars
I'll fly today to sunny shores.

I sit upon a pretty cloud,
as life below is much too loud,
but here I bask in rays of sun
a pretty cloud I sit upon.

I'm spreading wide my angel wings,
bid farewell to church bell rings,
I'll say goodbye to countryside,
my angel wings I'm spreading wide.

In floods of tears, I start to weep
as I await those lambs to leap,
when spring will take away my fears,
I start to weep in floods of tears.

Forgive our indiscretions

Try to take time in life to always pray,
pray for ourselves and others in our lives,
lives matter, in the chaos, we will die,
die for our indiscretions with our lies.

Lies bring the sorrow into people's hearts,
hearts heal inside a loving peaceful home,
home where we learn to curb our saddened words,
words said without a thought, we all have thrown.

Thrown every chance we had to bring the peace,
peace can begin to heal our wounds inside,
inside where pride and anger can renew,
Renew our tears, when all we did was try.

Forgive Yourself

When images reflect our own disgrace,
and tears begin to fall into the night,
forgiveness is a skill we must embrace.

As deeds have consequences that we face,
we learn that often we cannot be right,
when images reflect our own disgrace.

Someone we trusted raced to take our place,
our anger deep, to counteract in spite,
forgiveness is a skill we must embrace.

And when a grudge has left an acrid taste,
with conscience there begins a fearless fight,
when images reflect our own disgrace.

As power fame and money can't replace
a friendship lost because we dimmed the light,
forgiveness is a skill we must embrace.

When guilt consumes our heart and soul debase,
and grief within is bitterly contrite;
when images reflect our own disgrace,
forgiveness is a skill we must embrace.

Fractured Leadership

Gone are the days of Charles the first
we cannot use the axe,
and when our government is cursed,
they're like a plague of rats.

The arrogance in leadership,
has unconvincing vibes,
as empty words are tightly lipped,
and we have not subscribed.

So out of touch is his doctrine
this overbearing clown,
will lead our country into sin,
and all of us will drown.

Free as a Bird

On high we spy you from the sky,
you people there,
who cannot share,
for you are grounded, cannot fly,

or touch a cloud,
you're not allowed,

you have no springs, to see these things,
or be as free
you are not we,
for we are kings, as we have wings.

Fresh Cream Cakes

I can satisfy lust,
with my powerful cream,
once tasted, you will never look back!

In a moment of trust,
you'll be lost in a dream . . .
and you will not see the deadly attack;

as I tempt 'till you cry,
and for me you will buy,
as I pile every pound to your hips.

For my passion you'll die,
as you say your goodbye,
with your thought of me, still on your lips.

Friendship and Support

When the task has me beat
and I look to my friends,
they will see the defeat in my eyes.

Walk too far on these feet
and their healing depends,
on my loyal and trusted allies.

As good friends are aware
that we must join in force,
always help one another along,

for to share is to care,
on life's journey of course,
for support when we're not feeling strong.

"Christine Burrows"

Fun at the Fair

I had so much fun when the fair came to town,
as brightly lit rides took away my sad frown.
The giant machines took us spinning around
and music played loudly to drown out the sound.

My sister and I rode on every slide,
we then won a toy on the coconut shy,
we tasted the sweet fluffy sugary wool
of sticky floss candy, that made us feel full.

The carousel ride was my favourite spin,
those galloping horses with bright golden skin,
I will not forget, my great day at the fair
I treasured the moment, my sister was there!

And now looking back at the fun in the past,
a photo reminded, these moments don't last.

Gender Swap

There is a transformation that takes place
as age decides to trace another root,
replacing gender roles we must embrace,
identities are in some disrepute!

As women grow a beard, their voice is deep,
they also often weep, at loss of hair.
Of weaker muscles, men may often speak,
and fuller breasted chests with women share.

The gender swap means females now are males
and so they often fail to turn men's heads,
and scales are evened up when age curtails
men's manhood will not rise, it has been said.

Reversing roles mean women take control,
and men decide to just do as they're told!

Good Health

When failing health starts its descent,
the fun is spent
on borrowed time,
we're in decline.

The most important wealth we own
is not our phone!
To be unwell,
a kind of hell.

When healing brings a coloured cheek,
when health is peek,
the day will pass,
ill health won't last.

Good Timing

There once was a Poet with timing,
who wrote clever ditties whilst climbing,
securing his words
as meter's for nerds,
with shifts of sweet melody rhyming.

Goodbye Grey Skies

I left the skies of grey at home,
I'm not alone in chasing sun,
on foreign land I'm left to roam,
the whole adventure has begun.

Volcanic soil seems strangely tame,
without the rain, I think I've won,
a little bit of heaven claim,
the famed adventure has begun.

What's missing is the friendly talk,
the county walk, I miss the hum,
that English days of summer brought,
the short adventure brought the sun.

As winter grips the soil again,
returning when the grey is done,
I hope my memories remain,
proclaim adventures yet to come.

Goodbye Mrs May

Oh Mrs May what can I say,
I do love you!
The bastards would not let you stay
the time here flew . . .
You have my heart, you did your best
and from the start, you should have guessed
you took the fall for all the rest
and my heart grew.

Despite the flack, knives at your back
you stood well firm.
The house would often launch attack.
as we now learn:
The task in hand, impossible
now they hold you responsible,
the Brexit gate's unlockable,
it is their turn.

The Europeans won't back down
it is my view.
They do not want the UK crown
so they withdrew.
Now go write your biography
and let us be the referee
for me, you have my heart you see,
I do love you.

Goosing Around

Complaining geese make lots of noise,
they boss the ducks about;
I see them skim the pond, these boys,
who rule, and bite and shout.

The long necks of bad tempered males
lean forward to chastise;
they steer and balance with their tails,
and slap those they despise.

Collecting twigs and bark and leaves,
they use an old warm nest;
the males protect by any means,
devotion is expressed.

These geese are loyal to their mate,
and mourn, when there's a loss.
When left alone to widowed fate,
their sadness comes across.

This is inspired by my daily walk past Stowe Pool where I feed the geese and the ducks, they make a terrible racket every day and I see the males biting the other ducks showing them who is in charge. Evidently Geese mate for life and show emotion to each other and concern when one of them leaves.

Gossip Girl

There was an old woman from Lichfield
who spied everyone with her eyes peeled;
a rumour perverse
was penned in quick verse,
the chaos ensued with her lips sealed.

"Christine Burrows"

Green Apple Pie

Now I just love green apple pie,
I can't deny the taste;
so don't be shy give it a try,
oh my, I eat in haste.
A slice will take away your woes,
and satisfy down to your toes,
with ice-cream we can juxtapose,
pie never goes to waste.

"Dolly's Poetry Pudding"

Halloween Tricksters

Apparitions haunt
on chilly October night
masquerading their
scary imagination
ghoulish skeletal tricksters.

"Christine Burrows"

Heads Up

Purple crocus heads
poke snow to free their colour
spring wakes hopeful hearts.

HeatWave

Summer's heatwave melts
the fabric of my spirit,
lethargy consumes.

"Christine Burrows"

Her Star Eclipsed

"Please sing to me," my Mama said,
as she was sick and stayed in bed.
I sang my best and sweetest song,
to sleep she fell, she wasn't strong.

My memory now fades to grey,
as I remember that sad day,
the years we spent were all too short,
such precious jewels left in my thought.

Her final words had set her free,
"Please always sing that song to me."
As words were stolen from my lips,
on earth I saw her star eclipse.

Dedicated to my Mother who died 18th July 2014
I think about her often.

"Dolly's Poetry Pudding"

Hesitation

There's a lot riding
on cautious hesitation
to avoid a fall

"Christine Burrows"

HighWaymen

Beware the modern highwaymen,
on-line again;
no loaded guns
to withdraw funds.

These rough rogues are everywhere
they set their lair
under our skin
then we walk in.

When scamming us commands no fine,
their web design
is just a fake,
they steal our cake.

"Dolly's Poetry Pudding"

Hope

Hope,
ambitious seedlings
desirous of fulfilment

Contest winner

How Strange is Age?

Not sure how it has happened, but I see a different face?
When I look in the mirror now, of me there is no trace!
The person looking back at me has wrinkles and is old!
And something in my heart and soul has turned a little cold.

Inside my mind, I am still me, and I just feel the same,
and who is this imposter who is looking very plain?
Did time disintegrate me? Is this what they call age?
If this is true, then growing old can be so very strange.

My spirit has the strength of youth, my heart, has so much love,
my body wants to run a mile, my legs stick in the mud!
But I can see the generations, that my seed has sown,
a small price I have paid for this, my face has to atone.

I Caused a Stink

I pitched the product to the crowd
so loud was the applause!
My efforts made me very proud,
I vowed to stay the course.

And each time I presented there,
I tied myself in knots,
until the day I was aware
this chair called all the shots.

A slave to work I did become
the run was in my face,
succumbed to every drumming hum,
a rat within a race.

No time for me to see my friends
intention was to own,
and this is where the story ends,
I sent them back their phone.

Now I'm retired, I can now write,
a word about my plight,
the day left an empty chair,
that caused a stink in there.

I Forgive the Past

As I empower time, and waste an hour,
in contemplation of the life I've lived.
My memories in photographs devour,
my eyelids close, and thoughts begin to drift.

In every yesterday, history's cast,
the facts remain like sentinels in stone,
if only unsaid questions had been asked,
unanswered hidden deep, and never known.

But dwelling on the past is futile here,
there's hope in changes we can make tomorrow.
and not repeat the sins of yesteryear,
ensuring that the future has no sorrow.

Tomorrow's recollections will be best.
as saddened memories are put to rest.

Ilya Kuryakin

For those who remember the sixties,
this magical, sexy character appeared
on my old black and white TV!

He brought a welcomed sensuality to my life;
this spy, and hero of the Cold War.

This blonde Beatle was the man from U.N.C.L.E,
fulfilled all my dreams back then.

I was in love . . .

David McCallum you won my heart
with your soft soviet do-gooder voice
and innocent approach.

Where are you now, we miss you . . .

For those too young to remember, Ilya Kuryakin was a character played by David McCallum in the popular series shown on the TV during the 1960's called (The Man from U.N.C.L.E.) Of course they always won the battle and Ilya was innocently sexy. He was, of course English!

I'M MISSING YOU ...

I kept your secret safe within,
and didn't breathe a word;
and now your gone, your plunder done,
now life seems so absurd.

How can it be that you to me
like two peas in a pod;
and when one dies, as death defies
then all that's left, is God.

As long as life is in my heart,
I will remember thee,
we shared, we cared, and we were paired,
your secret's safe with me.

IMMORTALITY

If my heart should give out
whilst I'm sleeping in bed,
do not think of me gone from this world,
for my feud is devout,
to live on when I'm dead,
with the stroke of my pen's written word.
Here I lie underground,
but my soul is still near,
my emotions alive here today;
every word is profound,
of the love and the fear,
inside verses, life will not decay.

In Treasured Chests

In treasured chests there is much gold,
those memories so very old
the wealth of love in photographs
of those long gone and in the past
I feel their warmth, they've not been sold.

Now it's my turn to be enrolled,
the stories, poems I have told
include some books with autographs
in treasured chests.

In life I have been very bold,
experience is in my stroll
and in my heart I have amassed
a lot of special artefacts,
before too long they'll be consoled
in treasured chests.

INSOMNIAC

Deprived of sleep, he stayed awake all night,
insomnia, the curse that blights his day;
at dawn the tiredness, he could not fight.

Prepared for bed, he took a pill; despite
his eyes wide open, sights to still survey,
deprived of sleep, he stayed awake all night.

The rising of the sun brought in the light,
a yawn encompassed all he had to say,
at dawn the tiredness, he could not fight.

His body was a weak and feeble sight,
by day, a zombie was now on display,
deprived of sleep, he stayed awake all night,

refusing to lay down he stayed upright,
and walked and walked because he felt okay,
at dawn the tiredness, he could not fight.

His body clock would not conform, despite
the effort he put in to make it lay,
deprived of sleep, he stayed awake all night,
at dawn the tiredness, he could not fight.

Is There a God?

Is there a God when life is cruel
and hatred in our world has rule.
To ask the question, ask him why?
We pray with heads held to the sky.
Or am I just a silly fool?

My faith was tested when at school,
when bullied, my hot temper fuelled,
but when my prayer had no reply,
is there a God?

I always thought my church a jewel,
I learned to never start a duel,
so why do others fight and die,
and grieve and mourn, I hear their cry
as life can be so very cruel,
is there a God?

It's Daybreak

As mornings guarantee the light
and daybreak quells the long cold night.
The sun's warm shadow tells the time,
another day I claim as mine.
Appreciating hours on earth
    a bird will sing,
      the raindrops bring
    a touch of hope
    with lots of scope,
as new life has a chance to birth.

Another day to eat and drink,
be happy, and have time to think.
How lucky we are to be here,
I praise my day and give a cheer,
I love my life here now with you,
    I watch the moon,
    as all too soon
    the end will come
    and stop the fun,
but daybreak means I can renew.

Karate Chop

There was a young man who had wood,
and he wanted the pretty girl's bud;
her skill in karate,
then halted his party,
when her chop caught his horny manhood.

"Dolly's Poetry Pudding"

KiNg oF CriMe

He did not bring his knife today,
he left his hate at home.
He saw his Mother kneel and pray,
some faith he has now shown.

But once among his buddies there,
who threaten him with strife,
and make him on his honour swear
next time to bring his knife.

They mean to shed blood in the town
some innocent will die,
this gang where honour bears the crown,
and their rules will apply.

His destiny is set in stone,
on death row he'll be king.
For now he sits upon the throne,
electric cables ring.

Knife Crime

He wore designer trainers then,
his cap was back to front,
a cool dude in his track suit top
with fur around the hood.
Concealed inside is pocket was
a blade to pull his stunt.

His swanky walk and big boy talk,
his shoulders broad and strong,
and he believed that he could stalk,
his prey to him belonged.
His knife was quick, hit like a stick,
the stab was wide and long,

the victim fell and he could tell,
that death was imminent,
he stole the swag, the victims bag
left bare in sad lament.
The deed was done, he had to run,
and so he upped and went.

An orange suit now dons this brute.
a cell on death row's mile,
Now on a course with no remorse,
the sentence stole his smile.
A wasted life ruled by the knife,
because he was hostile.

Laws can Thwart Happiness

One thing that I have learned in life
we sometimes toe the line;
work through the system and the strife
we finely tune, define.

The mine field littered everywhere
with 'do's' and 'don'ts' abound,
The forms, the laws and where to swear
allegiance to the crown.

Our freedom is severely cut,
when navigating earth,
as who we are means doors are shut,
our birth place has great worth.

The fight goes on for human rights,
sometimes the laws are harsh.
The empathy for people's plight
dogged by a boggy marsh.

Learning From Experience

When truth is staring back at us,
and lies uncovered have deceived,
it's hard to then recover trust,
when all was lost when we believed.

But learning from our past mistakes,
survive another fateful day,
ensure our hearts will never break
protecting them from disarray.

When we're prepared for tearful cries,
avoid a painful destiny
of sorrow and of hurtful lies
to seek the purest honesty.

Then when the truth is staring back,
we've learned to know and recognise,
stand firm and strong in each attack,
internalise the exercise.

Learning From Love

We both enjoyed the company,
our love was true back then;
before our world began to change,
disdain reared up again.

In time respect was lost to us,
we did not see it come;
but love should bring us happiness
not make us want to run.

As time went by we grew apart,
our love began to die,
and we admit that this was it,
the final last goodbye;

and when you give a thought to us,
do not look back with rage,
as we have much to learn from this
before we turn the page.

Let Rip

The sailor lived near Barcelona,
he had a sweet natured persona,
but when he let rip,
his fart moved his ship,
all the way to Arizona!

Live in Happiness

Time is everything
the yellow brick road of fate
a long golden mile
seconds are wasted in doubt
leave memories in laughter.

Long Summer Days

The summer scene and in between
tree branches glint with sun.
The gentle breeze begins to tease,
with golden lights that stun.

The tranquil peace, as time decreased,
a slowing of the pace;
and all around would bless the ground,
appreciating space.

I stall and pause as I recall,
those summer days now past,
I played with friends when I was small,
how long they seemed to last.

Lost to US

He did not wear his soldier's coat,
for he had been disarmed;
and soon his mood became remote,
his fam'ly were alarmed.

Of warring days he did not speak
not one word did he say,
behind his eyes, there was a shriek
but cries were kept at bay.

And all the love left in his heart
encased within a capsule,
had been destroyed and torn apart.
infested was his castle.

A shell was left without a soul,
he could not tell us why,
in hopelessness, he lost control,
and life was passing by.

And deep within his lonely walk,
the flowers were not seen
though birds united in a squawk
his nightmare was so keen.

One day a girl tugged at his coat,
she'd lost her way back home,
before he spoke, he cleared his throat,
then said: "you're not alone."

Love Across the Miles

The months have flown without my lover here,
his heart was taken by the sea and sand,
no comforting of souls that we hold dear,
but may be soon we'll share all we have planned,
the months have flown without my lover here.

The summer season fills his heart with sun,
he walks the hills and valleys where he sleeps,
I wonder if inside his dreams I've won
a place within his precious heart for keeps?
The months have flown without my lover here.

Love Matters

It matters not the years
or the tears we've shed;
times we spent a toiling,
the lack of sleep in bed.

It matters not the loss
the loves, and fearful deaths
the guilt we felt inside
that left let us all bereft.

What matters here is time,
as life can be cut short
those memories we hold
that never can be bought.

It matters that we live
forgive, and keep our faith
retain hope in our hearts,
with love we'll not forsake.

Love Saved My Tears

Not seen your face in quite a while,
your big blues eyes are gone,
but I remember your neat style,
unique from everyone.

Old t-shirts would last donkeys years,
no rich designer clothes;
you chose sweet hearts, and saving tears,
and it was me you chose.

We shared so many special dreams,
you were my friend, my rock,
if I was broken at the seams,
you would then bear the shock.

You never said goodbye to me
farewells were not your thing,
you locked my heart and took the key,
it's you who made it sing.

"Dolly's Poetry Pudding"

Magical Moon Mapping

Mesmerising Moon
Moving Monotonously
Majestic Malaise

Man Up
(A Rap Song)

(The hook)
"Man up" *he said,*
as he left us
fatherless, his cowardice
was odourless and colourless,
left penniless
and now the loss don't bother us!

Now downright poor we fought for life
and in that strife we loved to fight
as trouble called
it was installed,
no right, no sight, we saw no light.

No one to care or share was there
to offer us a chair
or spare a thought
if we were caught
incarcerated in the pen and when
a lawyer pleaded
what we needed
was support, a place to breath-in.

The hook)
"Man up" *he said,*
as he left us
fatherless, his cowardice
was odourless and colourless,
left penniless
and now the loss don't bother us!

No guide in life we swore to own
a home to warm our chilling bone
and stealing, dealing was appealing
rough and ready and unfeeling,
now kneeling, praying to the ceiling.

On death row our life has ended
we're suspended, undefended
we offended, courts extended
ball and chain now recommended
looking back when we pretended,
fatherless we were unfriended.

The hook)
"Man up" *he said,*
as he left us
fatherless, his cowardice
was odourless and colourless,
left penniless
and now the loss don't bother us!

Margherita Pizza

There was a young woman maned Lisa,
who stuffed herself full of cheese pizza,
she could not resist,
hot slices of bliss,
her favourite was sweet Margherita.

Marilyn

She yearned to star on movie night,
be centre stage beneath the light,
this pretty flower, ripe and youthful,
soon become a girl who's useful,
in Hollywood where stars are made,
    her innocence
    and confidence,
    without pretence;
    her diligence,
exploited, in this masquerade.

Ingenuous, this flawless pearl,
excited like a little girl,
grew up to know how cold the tears,
as loneliness can blight careers,
destroy one's self esteem and fight,
    succumb to pills
    and drinking ills,
    the countless bills
    with no more frills
and death can bring the only light.

"Christine Burrows"

Mariposa Wings

Mariposa wings
from hairy bug to beauty
metamorphosis
fancy filigree passion
swirling lacy underskirts

Martyrs of the 17th Century

I will tell you a tale
of a treacherous deed,
where a man in his eighties would die;

as this priest was quite frail,
for their need he would bleed,
and because he was catholic he'd cry.

But the power was firm,
disembowelling was rife,
and the morbid scene bloody profound.

With the public affirm
lost his head to a knife,
with a cheer when his head hit the ground.

The blessed Father William Ward unfortunately was hung, drawn, and quartered in London on 26th July, 1641, at Tyburn, on the Feast of St Anne. He was 81 years old.

Hung, drawn and quartered was first introduced in 1352 in England for high treason. It was a cruel and vicious act, and one of the worst punishments that could be given to anyone considered a traitor. The victim would be hanged almost until the point of death, then castrated, disembowelled, beheaded and chopped into four pieces. Their remains would be displayed in prominent places across the country for all to see.

Mary Lost Her Head

So hesitant she signed her name,
the warrant was for death,
and she was named in history,
more tragic than Macbeth.

Her cousin, the anointed queen,
poor Mary lost her head;
for years she was held prisoner
so the rumours said.

But this would haunt Elizabeth
until her dying day,
inherited her father's will
no catholic would stay.

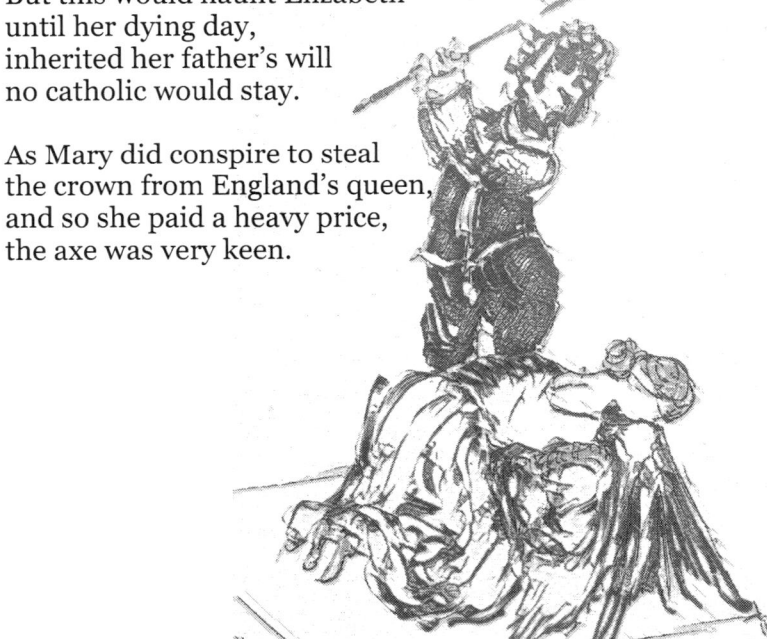

As Mary did conspire to steal
the crown from England's queen,
and so she paid a heavy price,
the axe was very keen.

Meet the Geriatrics

I'd joined the geriatric crew,
who need those sticks to help them bend,
my doctor took a diff'rent view,
on physio we should depend.

When bones are old, they stiffen up,
and creak like groaning ships at sea,
it happens to the best of us,
and stepping every day is key.

Keep moving with the times they say,
and don't succumb to moaning zones,
invest in new technology,
and throw away those flip-top phones!

Mental Illness

Inside the mind of anxious men
there lives a mission so intent,
oppressively the load is large
that strange behaviours are in charge.

No respite from the nervous bout
that makes a man begin to shout,
and fear can steer his mental state,
as anxious thoughts will not abate.

And soon the world is cold outside,
he thinks that everybody lied,
he trusts no one, not even those
who give their love, his heart has froze.

The isolation soon takes hold,
as all his love has now turned cold,
communication's lost with one
who cannot see his mind has gone.

Memoirs

I see the record of my life
in photos of the past,
and join those long lost relatives,
another didn't last.

Was that our Auntie Evelyn there,
with uncle Bill and Jim,
a long lost memory in time,
in albums stay within.

The clock will forge forever on,
no time to stop and think,
the past is just our history,
in photographs we shrink.

So whilst I can still take in breath,
I'll burn the midnight oil,
and write about adventures here
before I'm under soil.

Memories

Some magic had a hand in this,
the music sounds too good to miss,
as melodies reminded me
of when we both lived by the sea.
Now in the winter of our years
remembering
the past will cling
as voices sing
a bell will ring
and shadows will invite some tears.

Memories Inside My Heart

A change in season guarded by a chill,
and how unfair it is to dim the sun,
as raindrops trickle down my window sill,
I realise that gone is all the fun.

The bees have cleansed their knees and closed their eyes,
the squirrel hid his nuts inside his grin,
and trees have taken on a lean disguise,
by stripping every leaf from every limb.

And so the scene is set for cooler days;
the sale of summer shorts no longer thrive,
as woolly jumpers now are all the craze,
with Christmas cards sold in a pack of five!

Although I cry when sunny days depart,
I treasure memories inside my heart.

"Christine Burrows"

Merry Christmas and a Peaceful New Year

On Christmas Day I shout hurray,
as I will pray
a special birth
we leave our mirth.

To celebrate with our best friends,
our love extends
to everyone
we come upon.

On New Year's day I wish you luck
to have the pluck,
to keep the peace,
for war to cease.

Misguided Rain

As it rained throughout the day,
in a quandary, thoughts of May,
as heavens drench the little wren,
England's raining once again.

Playing with the puddles here,
little sun to please or cheer,
water spots on window panes,
wellie wearing in the lanes.

Thoroughfares reach breaking point,
flooding water now anoint,
overflowing with the mud,
this is not how summer's bud.

I am lacking season's cheer,
through the looking glass it's clear
smiles have left this face of mine,
now this lover's lost in rhyme.

As July here is steeped in sin,
I am now vexed, soaked to my skin,
turn back the clocks is what I say
please take me back to sunny May.

"Christine Burrows"

MISSING KISSING

If I could steal a thousand kisses
storing snogging for future times;
when loving I am missing
I'd take one to feel fine.
Alas so fleeting
kisses meeting;
lips now old
turning
cold.

Mixing Colours

There once was a young weaver from Leeds,
who mixed colour in beautiful themes
one day he saw red,
dye started to spread,
when the blues and the yellows made greens!

"Christine Burrows"

Mob Culture

Never argue with a pack
if alone they will attack
reasoning will cut no ice
as a mob will not think twice!

Blood is always what they want
as their fixed eyes, give much front
you are targeted for hate,
find the nearest exit gate.

Wicked wolves work good together,
with the tar, they always feather,
never is regret in mind,
only thoughts to be unkind.

Hanging mobsters get their man
sweet revenge is in their plan,
suffering will sooth the devil
inside evil they will revel.

Kings and Queens fall to the crowd
axing, cutting, they're not proud,
steer clear of vicious character,
mobs enjoy a vengeful massacre.

Monarch of the Glen

The monarch has an autumn wing
with gold and black fit for a king;
so richly deep against the sky,
this sovereign now in short supply.

As he displays his spots of white
a chequered flag is in my sight;
uniquely his display so sweet,
my eye appreciates the treat.

But life is short for pretty things
and to the greenery he clings,
and if you spot his dancing frills
they will excite inside with thrills.

This magic dancer flits and flaunts,
enjoy his mesmerising jaunt,
as soon this butterfly will die,
so never let this chance go by.

Moon Phases

In its glow, we watch the show
mooning cycles we all know
power rides, as it decides,
always pushing pulling tides.

Passionately holding tight
earthly beings see at night
fullest moon will shine on us,
never doubt how grandiose.

Lunar cycles count the days
all unseen, but strictly phased,
playing with our minds and thoughts
vowing that we'll be distraught.

Moons in the pink make us blink
loving moons in berry ink,
soothing amber glowing bright,
fools us that its sun at night.

If the moon should disappear,
nightly routines fall to fear,
control of all we've come to know,
end if moon decides to go.

Mocking Lies

Investing in the truth can burn some souls,
as there are those controlling with their lies,
their goals achieve much wealth among the bones
of those who maybe meek and ill advised.

The search means they endanger with their deeds,
as those who lie will feed on evil acts,
with greed they will protect as they succeed,
to hide the truth, concealing all the facts.

It is the brave who seek and also find,
as they are never blind or turn their eye,
behind the doors of power they're inclined,
to use their every skill to lurk and spy.

Deceit can sting with its ferocious fire,
one man's damn lie can kill with its desire.

My Car and Me

Now me and my old car
in need of tender care,
the twinkle in our star,
now has a little wear.

My filter needs a change,
my plugs have lost their power,
and faded paint looks strange
it's dull and drab and dour.

My sluggish starter motor
will splutter, spit and moan,
the slowest engine rotor
will always have a groan.

The tread worn down by miles,
unsteady is my grip,
and everybody smiles
when cloudy fumes emit.

This rot box is my friend,
we get from A to B,

together the 'till the end,
me and my car agree.

My Insomnia

I cannot sleep, it makes me weep,
as bright light through my curtains peep,
the sun is up, I'm wide awake,
and breakfast pancakes start to bake,
but I am tired, and feel so weak,

dark shadows under eyes are deep,
the wrinkles on my forehead creep.
I need a nap, for goodness sake,
I cannot sleep.

Now I am curled up in a heap,
and, from my dreams, I take a leap,
I'm shaken by the garden gate,
so now, again, I'm wide awake.
This tiredness I cannot beat,
I cannot sleep.

My New Philosophy on Life

I navigate the dross in life,
now flicking through its pages,
The do's the don'ts that bring me strife,
have thwarted me for ages.

Now that I've reached a ripe old age,
I can now turn away,
a whining voice, or moaning rage
dismissed into the fray.

I only let my eyes view good,
the bad does not compute.
My temper I keep under hood,
I'm never in dispute.

My chosen life is filled with dreams,
and every day is fine.
The world can go to pot it seems
I will not toe the line.

My Prince, My Knight

You have been here so many years,
I know because I've shed some tears,
when you were laid here long ago
I faced so many inner fears.

Since then I coped with rain and snow,
the grief of loss you'll never know
so glad you'll never know my pain,
I was ashamed to sink so low.

I learned to shelter from the rain,
to navigate and to contain
compose myself both day and night,
with confidence I have regained.

And now I use my pen to write,
I am at peace, my spirit bright,
this story of my prince, my knight
one day we both shall reunite.

"Christine Burrows"

My Velvet Treasure Troves

Hibiscus flowers
soft velvet colour petals
they eclipse my heart
don't camouflage your beauty
bequeath cherished treasure troves.

If you know Hibiscus, it flowers for just one day, which is sad, and then closes its petals to die, until another opens and sometimes two or three at a time if we are lucky, but the show is worth the wait.

Nature's Sound

Inside the wood
a peaceful solitude was found
inside the wood;
where sun kissed twinkles where I stood
caressed through leafy trees to ground,
a thumping rabbit makes a sound
inside the wood.

Some rabbits will thump one foot on the ground, some will thump both hind feet at the same time. Rabbits aren't very vocal so thumping is an important way of communicating. They may remain in the thumping posture until convinced that the danger has gone.

"Christine Burrows"

Naughty Ghosts in Purgatory

I hear the rattling of the chains,
the sound is all that still remains
of those who have been laid to rest,
but still in halls they haunt the guest.

For those who sinned there is no peace
and from their chains won't be released,
for they are paying high a price,
for those they cheated more than twice.

In purgatory they remain,
they forged in life this linking chain,
and so these ghosts will seek revenge,
by haunting those they think infringed.

So if you hear a clanging near,
stay in your bed and never fear,
these foolish ghosts can't hurt you now,
for they're in chains that disallow.

The racket that they make at night,
may give a few, a tiny fright,
but they're imprisoned by the hour,
and in their chains have little power.

I dedicate this to Dean Kuch who was the master of horror. Dean was a prolific poet from Georgetown Ohio, United States, who wrote his horror stories to chill us to the bone, often with a sense of humour and always a joy to read. He was a gentleman who always showed kindness in all his reviews. He will be greatly missed. Dean died in 2019. Rest in peace my dear friend.

No Switches

Confusing is the world today,
have humans really lost their way
so lazy now we have become,
we never want to switch things on!

The couch is where we want to stay,
robotic systems are in play,
our tongue is now a new mod-con,
we never want to switch things on!

Remote controls in automation
can this relieve our true vexation
those buttons obsolete, now gone!
we never want to switch things on!

And these machines can't understand,
how keenly constant our demand
sat in the dark, can't come upon
the switch to try to turn things on!

"Christine Burrows"

Noisy Days

A crash, a bang, a thumping noise,
my tranquil peace and calm destroys.
As nature's voices can't compete
with sounds of auto's in the street.
I yearn to hear a natural beat.
The birds at dawn are filled with joy
soon gone, when engines roar and toy.

A crane lifts girders to the sky,
another building built so high;
electric drills and hammers sound,
a digger burrows underground,
with clanging spans for miles around.
The birds at dawn are filled with joy
soon gone, when engines roar and toy.

Not So Funny

I had an old girlfriend called Honey,
whose boyfriend took all of her money;
so she sold his car,
and electric guitar.
and he didn't think it was funny.

"Christine Burrows"

Nothing Changes

When nothing changes; years go by,
the flowers grow, birds fly up high.
The skies are grey, the sun is shy,
we laugh and sing, we also cry.

Old buildings stay, when we are gone,
and nothing changes, time runs on,
to ash and dust we all succumb,
no one escapes the reaper's fun.

But human nature's just the same,
we all seek wealth and some seek fame,
and nothing changes life's sweet game,
we love, we hate, we all have shame.

We live in times of poverty
and sometimes life is fancy free,
injustices we often see,
but nothing changes you and me.

The only thing changing is our knowledge of the world, inventions, and technology, our human traits remain the same.

Oh Brenda

Oh Brenda did you see me standing there,
with tears in my eyes that we both share.
You took my husband and deceived your own,
all four of us are torn and now alone.

I cannot lay the blame on only you,
deceit is always shared between the two.
Now word has spread about you being paired,
I hope the loss is worth what you two shared.

And now betrayal's left its bitter scar,
my blood runs cold and black like sticky tar.
and painful daggers pierce inside my soul,
that left inside my heart an empty hole.

Oh Brenda, can't you see my love is real,
he means the world to me, I now appeal . . .
please give him back to me and walk away;
I will forgive you both in prayers today.

For you are young and pretty, eyes of blue,
cascading curls and ruby red lips too,
your legs are long, so gracious is your carriage,
please don't use your charms to wreck my marriage.

For what we've shared has been a bumpy ride,
and built on loving warmth we felt inside,
you'll cast this whim so carelessly aside,
and leave all love affairs for you that died.

Oh Brenda, hear my words, I'm pleading now,
release your hold and let him go somehow,
no other man for me will win my heart,
I promise I won't shoot . . . if you depart.

ON CHRISTMAS DAY

On Christmas Day I wake at dawn
I look for tracks upon my lawn.
Did Santa visit me last night,
was I asleep and missed the sight?
The sleigh was reindeer-drawn.

Today a baby boy was born
nativity our homes adorn,
and carols sung "Oh Silent Night,"
on Christmas Day.

We celebrate this special morn,
eat turkey, ham and piggies brawn.
The pretty fireworks ignite,
light up white snow to make it bright;
our flimsy paper hats are torn,
on Christmas Day.

ON ENGLAND'S SHORES

On England's shores we paddle feet,
wet muddy sand our print is neat,
tied handkerchieves upon our head
and rolled up is our trouser leg,
our happiness is then complete.

We love our fish and chips to eat,
the Punch and Judy show's a treat,
or we collect some shells instead
on England's shores.

The pier is where we take a seat
to watch the band play something sweet.
Feed seagulls with left over bread,
and to the local pub we tread,
to watch the sun on its retreat
on England's shores

"Christine Burrows"

On Foreign Soil

On foreign soil I find myself,
and fitting in this land of wealth,
accepting cultures not my own,
embracing customs on the phone,
the more I learn and gain in strength.

The sunny days are good for health,
and myths about this land dispel,
as here it feels so much like home,
on foreign soil.

With every intake of my breath,
the steps I take, improve my stealth;
on beaches and in forests comb,
to reach the summit on my own,
as here my talent will excel
on foreign soil.

"Dolly's Poetry Pudding"

Open Hearts

Love has thorns sometimes,
allow your heart to flower,
a rose holds much rain.

"Christine Burrows"

OrgaSMic

Though plastic is so artificial,
a dildo can be beneficial,
it won't fail to rise
its oomph never dies
and triumph is not superficial.

Over Sexed and Over Here!

The Yankee boys are coming, oversexed and over here,
that's what my Grandma used to say, in World War Two, me dear.

A pocket full of dollars and silk stockings for the girls,
their easy twang and slang . . . beguiling, charming pretty pearls.

The yanks here in the English towns, caused boys to moan and frown,
stealing kisses from the missus, in my Grandma's quiet town.

And some were wed, some took to bed by sexy Yankee boys,
some married, pregnant bellied, as they left their seeds of joys.

They strutted stuff, enticed enough, and whistled at the tarts.
The English rose with sullied clothes, were ruffled by the narks.

"Christine Burrows"

Painful Memories

As words fall to the page from inner thoughts,
I realise I'm caught in winds of time.
Aborting all attempts to reach the port,
I set myself adrift in life's sweet rhyme.

I waste my days on memories long gone,
so many hours of fun I can recall.
I shun the mounting age I've come upon
remembered in the photos on my wall.

The taste of stale regret lies on my tongue,
as in the sweetest song there is still doubt;
the wrongs that linger still feel very strong,
and chills within my spine begin to mount.

The past cannot be altered now to suit
some painful memories are still acute.

Past Loving Times

I miss you dear, you were sincere
your picture now reminds;
your smiles now are my souvenir
of kissing, loving times;
and when I sleep, I know you're there,
you whisper in my ear.
I know you care, with me you share
my heartfelt little tear.

Peace

A brand new start for the year ahead
as optimism flourishes
new ideas are given life
nourished by faith and hope
love and charity
the best ever
this New Year
promise
peace.

Perfect Christmas Chimes

When Christmas comes, we're full of celebration,
the sparkle decks our halls, we don't think twice
of time that's spent on all the preparation,
excitement's in our bones, we think it nice.

Each year the lights and tinsel will entice,
and fill our hearts with joy and jubilation;
our Christmas table gleams as it's precise
and we rejoice in all the exultation!

But why do some refuse participation?
Like Scrooge they will reject the season's spice,
dislike the hype, without an explanation,
the sparkle decks our halls, we don't think twice.

The roast we boast, the Christmas pud we slice,
the games, and all the disorganisation;
exhausting it may be to reach the heights,
but these events will build a firm foundation,

to pass the seed of joy down generations,
we praise the birth, as Jesus Christ invites
us all to share in this great admiration,
excitement's in our bones, we think it nice.

So join the throng, turn on your Christmas lights,
bring happiness in this anticipation,
it's only once a year, so be concise,
as here we have religious obligation
to Jesus, birth of Christ.

"Christine Burrows"

Perfect Roses

perfect
roses rescue
sad hearts

Perfumed Attraction

The fragrance wafted in the breeze,
a scent that's faintly Japanese,
and climbing high against the wall
attracting insects very small,
this yellow Jasmine sweetly clings.
The bee will hum
and more will come
to pollinate,
accommodate,
attraction's petalled charming wings.

And on my walk I pass them by,
the bouquet is in good supply,
this aromatic pungent whiff,
the pleasure is in every sniff
a bee begins to buzz about
his shimmy sways
with pollen plays
aroma flows
right up his nose . . .
this bumble bee's a clever scout.

"Christine Burrows"

Perky Poetry

Perfect Poetry
Pickled in Pessimism
Plagues NEW Prospectors

Pivoting Petals

Pivot of petals
a dance among the roses
a brief encounter
so many dreams to fulfil
before death kills pretty things.

"Christine Burrows"

Please Help?

I tried to call, but no reply
and this is why I said goodbye.
Machines that said, "I'll soon be there!"
But no one came on line to share,
frustrations high, my bitter cry . . .
I kept on asking myself why?
Why did I even want to try!
I didn't stand a single prayer
I tried to call.

Just one more client left to die
to hang onto the phone and sigh,
and left in utter deep despair;
no, not another questionnaire?
I need some help with my supply?
I tried to call!

Poor Granny

There was an old lady, a Granny,
and surgeons had tightened her fanny
no man could get in
the hole was too thin
retired was her nook and cranny.

"Christine Burrows"

Quentin, I Love you!

Old Quentin Crisp, he loved gay rights!
Sometimes he'd get into a fight,
in days when wearing pink forbidden,
he sometimes kept his maleness hidden.
Parading in his peacock hat,
he walked with pride and all of that.
So gay and proud and very loud,
and sometimes he'd attract a crowd.

His wisdom was unique on life,
his first rule was to flee from strife,
although he courted hell in town,
when he wore his Queenie crown.
I loved his attitude to dust,
he'd let it settle, never fussed!
"Don't waste time on cleaning house,
ignore the dirt, ignore the louse."

I liked his clear philosophy,
he saw the fun, and that was key.
He didn't think much of his crime
he died in nineteen ninety-nine.
He suffered taunts, was beaten up
and he was such a powder puff,
I loved you Quentin, you're a star
I send my message from afar . . .

you naked civil servant you,
a gem among the very few,
a di'mond shining in the dirt,
a fairy and amazing flirt!

Born Denis Charles Pratt, Quintin Crisp, an English openly gay man who wore flamboyant clothing and had an air of superiority, as men felt threatened by his openly gay appearance. He was beaten in the streets for being gay. He was gay at a time when it was illegal but he was brave and bold and courageous in my opinion. I loved his philosophy on cleaning, I spend half my life cleaning my house!

Rainy June

When clouds release a mighty storm
no sun in June
or shiny moon
is visible whilst rain drops form.

I pray some blue
will soon poke through.

The sodden soil is soaking wet
and roots deep down,
begin to drown
as seeds don't swim when under threat.

Rectified Dysfunction

A man with erectile dysfunction,
has slow and insipid eruption,
to help it stay up
a bicycle pump
will soon have a girl up the junction.

Revenge is Sweet

She never mentioned him to me,
unfaithful man.
Was not a fan,
her tears were all that I could see.

A broken heart
he did impart,

and mending wounds would take some time;
but she was fine,
we drank some wine,
and planned revenge for this 'ere crime.

RIP on the Streets
A Rap Song

(The Hook)
I was born on the streets

it ain't livin'

and the powers that be

ain't forgivin

the thugs who do drugs,
bear grudges because

I ain't doing that shit,

I'm still winnin.

I need to be left with a chance,
I ain't gonna die in a trance,
I'll tell you one thing,
It's me who can sing
and me, I get lost in the dance.

I ain't done no crime for a dime,
but my soul is ready to chime,
the beat keeps me warm,
my coat is still torn,
but I still got skill in me rhyme.

(The Hook)
I was born on the streets

it ain't livin'

and the powers that be

ain't forgivin

the thugs who do drugs,
bear grudges because

I ain't doing that shit,

I'm still winnin.

"Dolly's Poetry Pudding"

I never believe in tomorrow
today, I will beg, steal or borrow
I believe in my life,

I don't own a knife
and I won't succumb to no sorrow.

Don't judge me when you pass me by
for I can still reach for the sky,
cuz I'm not your kind,
in your stubborn mind,
believe only your rules apply.

(The Hook)
I was born on the streets

it ain't livin'

and the powers that be

ain't forgivin

the thugs who do drugs,
bear grudges because

I ain't doing that shit,

I'm still winnin.

RUTH

Ruth fell in love, and so thereof,
forever was her kiss;
and destined was their deadly path,
that neither could dismiss.

This boy at play would have to pay,
she would not be denied,
discarded for another girl,
and Ruth was full of pride.

A loaded Smith and Wesson shot
a bullet to his chest.
Ruth's stern determination meant
this boy would get the best.

In pools of blood he lay, she stood
and fired three more rounds;
and as he took his final breath
her knees fell to the ground.

And to the gallows Ruth was sent
she paid her debt in full,
the lovers linked by love and death,
her neck would feel the pull.

This woman was the last to hang,
went down in history,
she was deranged and it is strange,
to learn this mystery.

Ruth Ellis born 9 October 1926, died 13 July 1955. She was a British model and nightclub hostess. Ruth was the last woman to be hanged in the United Kingdom, after being convicted of the murder of her lover, David Blakely. She would have had the defence of diminished responsibility in today's court, but not back then.

Sad News

Braced in my chair tightly, I held my breath,
as the news determined a life or a death;
blood drained from my face, on hearing the answer,
partners no more, but alone was this dancer;
picking up pieces of lives that were left,
smiling so sweetly, all sorrow suppressed.

Bravely we forged toward what was to come,
neither would mention the death of life's drum;
natural process then followed in order
knowing we all were quite close to the border,
when the time came to kiss fam'ly goodbye,
blatant refusal was in his last sigh.

Salute the Red Admiral

This adm'ral of the insect fleet
complete with suit of red.
A squadron leader he entreats
his wings are fully spread.

And ready are his troops in line,
inclining pods await.
The garrison hang tight, resigned
to face a date with fate.

As they emerge from their cocoon,
they soon salute their king;
this stalwart of the red platoon,
queue up in early spring.

This chief of staff is resolute,
salute him, for he's proud.
His wings, a perfect parachute,
to please the waiting crowd.

Santa Indulges

Now Santa got merry on sherry
and Rudolf's red nose was contrary!
The elves ran amok,
the clock would not stop
his sleigh may not get to the Prairie?

Now Santa ate too many mince pies
and his belly's so heavy . . . he cries.
his red coat won't fit
his temper is lit
and tonight he may have to tell lies.

But we won't accept his excuses
a detox may stop his abuses
a diet tonight
enables the flight.
His sleigh was then be put to good uses.

Santa Likes a Curry

Now at Christmas the man dressed in red
leaves his gifts at the foot of our bed,
on the eve of the day
on the way to Bombay
he popped in for a curry instead.

School Days

A battered satchel was the rule,
graffiti daubed with pen.
John, Paul, George and Ringo drool,
I was a fan back then.

A pleated hoiked up skirt I dared,
to show my skinny pins,
I'd wear unsexy underwear,
my bare legs paid for sins.

My 'C' cup wonder bra I swore
enticed the boys out there,
I was a girl, right to the core
I had a lot to share.

Back then it was about the sex,
the flicks, the club, the snogging,
and school was really second best,
the music really rocking.

So did I learn to read and write?
A question you might ask.
The drama group was in my sight,
Bet Davies had my heart.

Some books I read left me quite cold,
the world was still in wait,
I never thought of growing old,
or what would be my fate.

I saw much violence in my school,
dished out by adult men,
to all the kids they were quite cruel,
the cane ruled over pen.

When I look back, I learned to show
a little more compassion;
this is the only way to know,
your heart has any passion.

"Christine Burrows"

Seasoned Reality

Stark trees bare their souls
prepared for frosty seizure
the strongest survive

Second Hand Rose

You look so awfully pretty
in charity bought frocks;
a hat bought from a market stall
and fifty pence white socks;

you look so bloody marvellous,
and darling you did well,
by saving all those pennies . . .
on second hand Chanel!

At Ascot all those heads will turn
in the clothes you chose,
no one would guess that your attire
was used before, dear Rose;

and I will keep your secret safe,
for no one will I tell,
you look a million dollars dear,
I'm envious as hell.

Serengeti

The lioness has cubs to feed,
they're all in need;
not for the thrill,
she has to kill,

as hunger bares its teeth to flesh,
a meal so fresh;
the kill is quick,
a tasty lick.

But others waiting in the wings
hyenas sing
and steal her prize,
to fight not wise.

Often Lions who make a killing only to have a pack of hyenas steal the meal, as the lioness who has cubs to feed will back off because she is outnumbered. Life is harsh in Serengeti.

Shadows

As shadows leave their stain on earth
that follow objects, make them birth,
it's light that casts the silhouette,
without which no reflection's set,
this partnership of light and dark,
    a dancing treat,
    to move our feet,
    and watch the show,
    of shadows glow,
that make us tall within the park.

And as the sun sets on our day,
the shadow of the moon at play,
now sinister, the mood has changed,
as shadows now have rearranged;
the figures will begin to haunt;
    a blackened ghost,
    within a cloak,
    a tree branch moves,
    and will confuse,
imagination wild, will taunt.

Shot For Love

She lurked inside the darkness of the night,
as shadows on the wall meant certain danger.
A man approached, his pistol he held tight,
but she was not afraid of this mean stranger.

Behind a trail of smoke, she calmly spoke,
"My business here for pleasure, not for pain."
As he relaxed, his interest awoke,
her smile and sexy voice took all the rain.

But he had no idea of her mission,
she drew the lamb into the lion's den,
intention here, to gain a good position,
her curves had mesmerised so many men.

When he was close she took his world apart,
as Cupid's arrow shot him through the heart.

Sleep Deprived

The night
is very long
and distant are our dreams,
as eyes refuse to rest in peace,
no sleep.

"Christine Burrows"

Smelling the Roses

The tickle of a perfumed rose,
a petalled musk
that I can trust,
went sensitively up my nose;

a talcum smell
creates a spell

and soon transported me inside
to summer calm,
a fragrant balm
has liberally been applied.

Smooth as Butter

I once knew a man with a stutter,
who chewed every word he did utter.
a croissant of note,
got stuck in his throat,
and words began melting like butter.

Snow and Ice

With icy snow, there could be fun,
to slide on the toboggan run.
Be careful as you fall below,
there could be fun with icy snow.

If you fall down, and break a leg,
you'll spend a lot of time in bed,
in winter you may wear a frown
and break a leg if you fall down.

With fur lined shoes, keep out the cold
especially if your bones are old,
don't let the chill bring on the blues,
keep out the cold with fur lined shoes.

The snow and ice, it's not that nice,
a tot of whisky might suffice.
The pretty scene cannot entice,
it's not that nice, the snow and ice.

Some Will Hang

A bullet shot from pointed gun
toward her lovers heart to stun.
This was a deathly evil plot,
from pointed gun, a bullet shot.

As he lay down on stony ground,
the murder clearly quite profound,
her broken heart would start to pound
on stony ground, as he lay down.

Ruth had to hang for this bad crime
there was no plea for prison time.
The solemn bells of Saint Luke's rang,
for this bad crime, Ruth had to hang.

Ruth Ellis was the last woman to hang in Britain on 13th July 1955, she shot her lover with a .38 calibre Smith & Wesson Victory model revolver, because, David Blakely had betrayed her. She hung at Holloway prison.

"Christine Burrows"

Storms

My tent of blue
is shrouded by black cloud
I'll soon be bruised.

Strawberry Tarts

The sun sets on a day of toil
strawberries ripe
a pretty sight
and tasty jam is on the boil.

sweet simmered treats
when winter's bleak

preserved in jars fresh from the store
to warm our hearts
we eat jam tarts
from summer season's laboured chore.

Stubborn

There was an old man with a grudge,
whose perspective would often misjudge,
his bitter hate
would not dissipate,
and his resolute rant would not budge.

Stunk Like a Skunk

There was an old man from Peru,
who wouldn't sit down for a poo.
It ran down his leg
resembled an egg,
he stunk like a skunk, this is true!

"Christine Burrows"

Summer Scenes

When seeds are sown and plants are growing
flowers bloom with nature knowing
colour brightens every scene
and fragrant roses dream
sweet scent is flowing
with happy beams
trees are green
colours
keen.

Sunny Roses

With floral fragrance
my sunny yellow roses
fill my room with spring.

Sweet Dandelions – The Happy Weed

The dandelion seed is strong
awaiting winds anew,
a parachute, a wealthy song,
another weed debut.

This yellow flowering curs-ed gem
transforms into white fluff,
the magic seed from every stem
is waiting for a puff.

This vintage ritual is pure
we blow to make a wish,
without a care we help procure
we blow their sweetest kiss.

The pretty floating feathered seed
to pastures new will hide;
until they spring to life with speed,
in yellow blooming pride.

Sweet Valentine

Sophisticated girl who stole his heart,
Without a word she'd silence any room.
Exciting, tantalising, from the start,
Evoking all who smelt her sweet perfume.
Tongues wagged and rumours spread about her life,

Vain accusations with no real foundation.
A word can spread to damn someone to strife,
Let envy rise with jealous incantation.
Events turned out to be in her best favour,
No one could tarnish hearts so full of gold,
Together they were happy, life to savour,
Inside their nest their love was never cold.
No man could separate these two love birds,
Enticing were their sweet and loving words.

"Christine Burrows"

Take a Walk With Nature

There's so much nature we can share
if we take time to get out there,
and use our feet to walk around,
to hear the birdies chirping sound.

To see the flowers in full bloom,
and watch the movement of the moon,
or maybe lie on fresh cut grass,
or simply watch the people pass.

Unwind, relax, appreciate,
as nature starts to compensate
with rain to water shrubs and trees,
and spreading dew to feed the bees.

So spare sometime to breathe the air,
there's so much nature we can share.

Take Care

Stop!
Look before you leap
or forever weep . . .
life can vanish inside a heartbeat!

Tell the Truth

Injustice grates within the heart
until fair play
has had its day
and truth prevails, if we are smart.

In wigs and gowns,
the ups and downs.

We navigate the devil's lair
uncover lies,
when courts advise:
on oath the truth we swear to share.

Tempestuousness

When sparks of temper rage like stormy seas,
and nothing quells the monsoon when it soars,
our hearts will paralyse into a freeze.

No sense in soothing anger into ease
inside a hurricane, the power stores;
when sparks of temper rage like stormy seas.

As fury in a breeze, can ruffle trees
and shake foundations with its mighty wars,
our hearts will paralyse into a freeze.

We build a sturdy house with expertise,
protect ourselves from waves that hit the shores,
when sparks of temper rage like stormy seas.

No freedom inside fear, we feel the squeeze,
a battle without hope of open doors . . .
our hearts will paralyse into a freeze.

And so we regulate and enforce laws,
to break resentment . . . rooting out the cause;
when sparks of temper rage like stormy seas,
our hearts will paralyse into a freeze.

"Christine Burrows"

Temptation

Temptation: how hard can I fight it?
With many treats out there to eat.
And pounds of fat cling tightly
too porky rounded seat.
I curse the baker!
Give **IT** to me
a d r e a m y
fresh cream
CAKE!

Tнat FateFuL Day

The dreaded hand that would not wait
and she could not anticipate,
as love consumed her loving heart,
she yearned when they had been apart.

But when his hand hit her face hard
she kept a proud and fake facade,
pretending his love still consumed,
but truthfully their love was doomed.

What would she do if left alone,
with kids to feed, her cover blown,
so on that fateful day she stayed
her faith in God, alone she prayed.

He came home drunk, and took a knife,
she didn't have a chance at life;
detectives knew they'd seen her tomb,
when luminol lit up the room.

Luminol is used to detect blood traces and is used by detectives at crime scenes.

"Christine Burrows"

The Battle Scars - 1914 - 1918

All England's watching you, the sergeant said,
as bayonets fixed, we sat behind the line,
in trenches with a tin hat on our head,
and puffing with great joy on our woodbine.

We'd handed in our photographs and letters,
they were kept to send on to our home,
as death was certain, they were taking measures,
the only item on me, was a comb.

The tanks manoeuvred first into position,
then next the trenches we would top,
the back-up team included a physician,
lest some of us be wounded, some would drop.

Bombardment shook the earth, the noise was loud,
"do not look back lads or you will be shot;
for king and country please be brave and proud",
and men cried for their mothers on the spot.

We strolled along the field amid the noise,
the rationed rum had lingered on my breath.
The war made men of all the younger boys,
as one by one they fell down to their death.

"Dolly's Poetry Pudding"

Faced with the end of life, I heard the screams,
survivors left to rot as bullets rained,
and many men sunk into muddy streams,
as silence fell among the bloody stains.

And Lilly of the Valley grew in mud
the beauty of the Camberwell in view,
the final push meant war was understood,
to end all wars, if only that were true?

The brave and wounded soldiers were alone,
not one man ever questioned or asked why?
Not welcomed back to jobs when they got home,
and no ex-service men need to apply.

After surviving this terrible war, these soldiers returned home and no one wanted to know about their experiences as there was little understanding of the effects of war. There was high unemployment and no one wanted to employ ex-servicemen as they obviously had some mental health issues due to the trauma of war. Men who fought for their country and suffered the loss of their friends were now very alone.

The BIG Guys aLWays WIN

What happened to the retailers?
They grew too big to even care;
this luckless band of new traders
the customer out there, beware.

Their practices firm to the core,
will fleece your purse of all its gold;
take care when buying goods in store
keep paper proof, or be controlled.

Take pictures when you're checking out,
ensure that purchases were bought
for if the goods not strong and stout
your money they have truly sought!

I learned a lesson here and there,
a credit note was all they gave,
now I am forced to shop back where
I have become their shopping slave!

The Botticelli Bather

He watched her silky curves as she was bathing,
a Botticelli innocent sweet girl;
a view so satisfyingly retaining,
he wished to know and love this pure white pearl.

He yearned to hear her speak and say his name,
to kiss those luscious lips and see her smile,
and hold her close and touch her fragile frame,
without her clothes she had the greatest style.

Alas he was beguiled by all her beauty,
a vision he would rather dwell upon,
to break the magic was beyond his duty
a pauper never wins a graceful swan.

Contented here in sweetest admiration,
enjoying soothing fine infatuation.

"Christine Burrows"

The Britishers

I lied about my age, they didn't mind,
at sixteen I was ready for the fight,
to kill the Jerrys we all had a mind,
and go to war, enlisting was our right.
A motley crew of unfit men were we,
with putties on and bayonets in our hand;
the Enfield was the closest friend to me,
we trained to plunge it deep in bags of sand.

We boarded boats and waved goodbye to smiles,
and Belgium was awaiting our attack.
On bread and Ticklers jam we walked for miles,
one hundred pounds was strapped to every back.
The shock of dereliction in the towns,
had stunted trees and buildings had collapsed,
the sound of whizzing shells was all around,
the rapid firing thuds of deadly traps.

In mud and dirty holes we were not vexed
though bloody stench of death would chill our bone,
at any time we knew we could be next,
in wet dug-outs we'd see our journey home.
Inside the trench, a brew was just the ticket
a slice of bullied beef served from the tin
then back to being hunted like a rabbit,
as men hung on the wire, flesh and skin.

We were united in the hobs of hell,
this camping holiday where men would play,
amid the rotting corpses we could tell
that life was short, our turn would come one day.
It was a long way from Tipperary
and in this boggy sewer we had fun,
as life and death were extraordinary
and linked with fate we knew our day would come.

Putties: bandage for a covering for the lower part of the leg from the ankle to the knee, alternatively known as: leg-wraps, leg bindings.

The Chime Operandi (Poetic Chimes)

This rhyming verse just may appeal
with zeal it rhymes with pride.
It pops inside to make you feel
that poetry can glide.
To sing with clever sounding words,
to feel the chime,
internal rhyme,
can be a sign
I'm in decline . . .
a crime to join poetic nerds.

"Christine Burrows"

The Cleaners

The fete is over, what a mess
is left to clear
no helpers here,
just me and you to have success.

The plastic bags
and nub end fags

are gathered with a caring hand
as soldiers who
like me and you,
our services are in demand.

The Cockroach Education Seminar

The bastards have insecticides,
your eyes will sting from it,
and every bit of strength provides
your chance to then transmit:
release the germs upon the floor,
all you have stored,
leave by the door,
heave from the core,
the spray ignore,
before you die, you score once more!

Your homework for this week is clear
appearances are key,
as humans see too well my dear,
your task this week will be:
to hide where you will not be seen:
a high bookshelf
conceal yourself,
improve your stealth,
safeguard your health,
and help yourself to their cuisine.

The Cycle of Life

When Sunshine creeps at dawn,
it glows on every bloom;
when sunset fades upon the lawn,
the buds reach for the moon.
The cloud burst sheds the rain
to water every seed,
and life is quenched upon the plain,
as every leaf will feed;
and deep inside the earth
roots spread their tiny feet,
as nature swears, with all her worth,
that life will be complete.

"Dolly's Poetry Pudding"

The Dance of the Ostrich

He hears the music in his head
and sees his Princess Queen,
his feathered fans are widely spread,
he's glad his plumes were preened.

Her elegance, a match for him
his dance will mean they're paired.
His claws now swiftly guide each limb,
he looks like Fred Astaire!

His feathers flapping to and fro
she is so well impressed;
he wins her love which starts to glow,
now they will build a nest.

The Dangerous Past

The peril of history thwarts our sunrise
with skeletal ghosts of the past;
regret in the sorrow cannot be revised,
the future's already been cast.

The errors in life leave a stain on our hands
we cannot remove it somehow;
when memories flood with a thousand commands
we're caught by a war we allow.

Now dragged by our hair into the abyss
the door to the future is closed;
the chains and the shackles preventing the kiss
that hearts would prefer to propose.

The spiralling down, will not be prevented
believing the guilt we observe,
to suffer our sins, so that we're repented
the silence is what we deserve.

And if we let go of the angst of the past
we'd fly like a bird, to the sky;
refusing to dwell on mistakes we've amassed,
we all can renew, if we try.

The Dawn Chorus

My favourite time of day is here
the early cheer of dawn,
when feathered friends are always near,
I hear their song each morn.
Intuitively they will start
to chirp a melody of art:
these clever birds are very smart.
and to my heart are drawn.

The Drug Dealer

He's on a roll, on his patrol,
with street cred . . . or he's fucking dead,
from head to toe, he is on show,
his muscles maxed to heir plateau
with street cred . . . or he'd fucking dead.

His screwed up dud is also shrewd,
and dealing crack is where he's at,
he packs a gun, it's not for fun,
a thirty-eight affects his gait,
this screwed up dud is also shrewd,

Steer clear in fear when he is near,
his eagle eye on you will spy,
he is on top, he spots a cop,
behind his shades his trade invades,
steer clear in fear when he is near.

The Earth, Moon and Sun

Forever phasing, waxing, waning,
the moon is on patrol;
as dark night skies are playing ball,
the white moon's in control.
And shadowed by her friend, the sun,
in space they fool around,
and gravitate in unison,
to earth they have been bound.
Without their toil, the earth would spoil,
would die without these friends,
they play their part, as they can chart,
on cycles, life depends.

The Fateful Flanders Fields

The silence fell upon the field,
the poppy yields to wind.
And as the gentle breeze appealed,
death healed all those who'd sinned.
No more mills bombs or rifle fire,
no squelch of boot in this quagmire,
just bodies hanging on the wire,
the Flanders mire now dimmed.

As life's so close to death it seems,
the line crossed keenly here,
the sacrifice of boys in teens,
the theme of war was clear.
you shoot to kill until your dead,
then when you lay your beaten head,
and face your maker with some dread,
the heroes shed their tear.

The battle fails to be a win
when men within are cold,
as victory is very thin
when kith and kin are sold,
they died a certain fatal death,
as each one took their final breath,
the senseless slaughter took effect
with much regret, it's told.

The Field of War

The field in spooky silence, is at rest,
for it has toiled to test its firm resolve,
an estimate of death it saw the best
and worst of human nature here dissolve.

This land has witnessed tragedy and sorrow
and here where life was borrowed in a breath
tomorrows stolen, as each man had followed
a path that took them to an early death.

Now gentle breezes sway the poppies there,
as if the peace was shared in years gone by,
the air is pure and fresh and lifts my hair,
and I cannot believe young men could die.

The tragedy of war is on repeat,
so many men will die in this deceit.

The Food Chain

We need to eat while we're awake,
we make a fluffy corn pancake,
our eggs are over-easy now
we never ask the why or how?
As nature gives, and we partake.

The fruit we pick from trees we shake
to make the apple pies we bake.
We need a drink, we milk the cow.
We need to eat.

We kill the cow and eat the steak,
for man's requirements he'll forsake,
when we're in need we want it now
as nature always gives somehow
we're in control, it's so opaque,
we need to eat.

The Get Away

If I could fly just like a bird
and be transferred
to fields of green
and waters clean.

Be free to breathe the country air,
without a care
as birds can choose,
to change their views.

If I could grow some angel wings,
I'd pack my things
and leave behind
the daily grind.

The Hospital of Doom

The hospital is hard and cold
an unfamiliar scene.
The reaper lurks to seek and hold,
his eye is mean and keen.

Some try to dodge, and circumvent
and hide behind a screen,
but when the time comes to repent,
no one will hear the scream.

Once entering those double doors,
all life is left to fate,
a place where there is no applause
our status makes us late.

More souls go in, and few come out,
a threshold of great doom,
no matter what they shout about,
death seizes all too soon.

The Irish Question

There was an old man from Killarney
who spent his time fighting the army
he would not enlist
instead he got pissed
so drunk he was full of the blarney.

The Lichfield Bower

The Bower draws the people here,
to picnic park
shared with the lark
a celebration every year

of special food
sweet smells exude.

A self-indulgent atmosphere,
kids will play
enjoy the day
and cheer the clever puppeteer!

The Lichfield Bower will takes place this weekend, hot food is sold on the streets from around the world, there is entertainment, puppet shows, bands playing and family picnics, the crowds come and enjoy the day.

The Lover's Brew

Bubble, bubble, boiled and fuddled,
passions burn within a cuddle.
Lust is thrown into the bake,
a caldron hot and trouble make;
cast a spell, and bring the fog,
stir in doubt and write a blog,
add a jealous word to sting,
take a lover, have a fling.
Rumours fly and tempers bubble
secret lies among the rubble.

Bubble, bubble boiled and fuddled,
passions burn within a cuddle,
cool it with betrayal's blood,
as lover's are misunderstood.

"Christine Burrows"

The Marriage Bond

A bond of ten long loving years
amid some tears
there have been cheers,
a new house opens new frontiers;

the strength within
with kith and kin

means conquering all coming strife,
you can resort
to good support,
as unity builds solid life.

For Emma and Adam

The Moon Remembers

The moon, it seems will come and go,
as time goes by, I've come to know,
it changes shape, and just for fun,
enjoys to run and chase the sun,
and shines its light on Mother Earth.
   Waxing, waning,
     misbehaving,
   it's out of view
   when it is new
remembering to then rebirth.

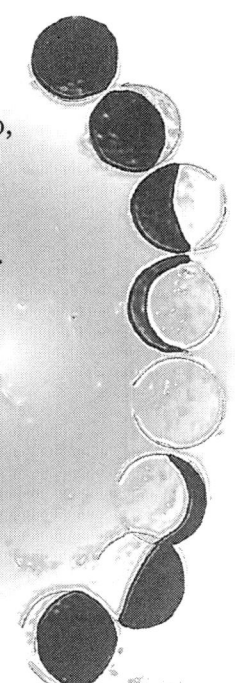

The Old Soldier

A shadow of his former self,
he stood so thin and pale.
A far cry from the battlefield,
where muck and bullets hailed.

Now old and frail, just skin and bone,
with no command inside.
With weakened steps he hesitates,
but still he has his pride.

He lived to tell his tale to us,
survived among his men;
he served his country, duty bound,
reported with his pen.

They dress him in his uniform
his medals weigh him down,
and he salutes in memory
of those now not around.

The Perfect Feminist

I am the perfect feminist,
I always know I'm blessed.
My attributes, the very best,
I've put them to the test.

As men are putty in my hands,
I make them do handstands.
They all succumb to my demands,
of me they are all fans.

I keep my secrets hidden well,
and never share or tell.
All females have that magic spell,
so use it to compel.

To all the girls I shout "Amen"
by rhyming with this pen.
Now take advantage of those men,
they're suckers for a hen.

The Power of Money

Money has the greatest power
to make our life secure,
but it can rule and it can sour,
and it can make us poor.

To prosper means we will commit
to riches we procure;
is evil at the root of it
not always is it pure?

Does money make us happier,
than someone without much?
Make us smart, or snappier,
can it become a crutch?

So necessary are bank notes
to pay for daily bread,
although love wins my heartfelt vote,
the money rules instead.

The Power of Poetry

If I give you a star
for your poem tonight
then your words found a place in my heart.

I am touched from afar,
by your guiding bright light,
and you influenced with your great art.

As your muse shone its torch
into my lonely life,
I then let you come into my world.

I can rock on my porch,
gone is grief and all strife,
when the poet so sweetly observed.

"Christine Burrows"

The Prowling Vampire

With garlic breath I lay in wait,
for vampire teeth are sharp,
as I agreed to be the bait,
to drive wood through his heart.

The air was still, there was no sound,
though I could feel a chill,
and from a coffin in the ground,
this monster I would kill.

My eyes began to fall asleep,
and into slumber fell,
no nightmare in my mind would creep,
of such impending hell.

Then suddenly I felt a pain,
so deeply in my neck,
and I was wide awake again,
I felt the icy breath.

As blood was drawn, I felt so weak,
like putty in his arms,
this vampire kissed me on the cheek,
succumbed was I to charms.

Incisors sharpened to a point,
my bite now clean as knives,
I prowl at night and will anoint,
I'm one of many wives.

So be aware that garlic breath
will never put me off,
and I can smell the blood of death
before you even cough!

Now I have joined the sisterhood,
I'll find you in your bed,
as cunning as a fox, I'm good,
I live among the dead.

The Rise of the Nazis

When poverty means people starve,
they look for earnest change.
Like sheep they will be lead to chart
a path that may be strange.

Then power goes to evil men,
who feather their own nest,
a change consumes, begins again
the start of great unrest.

An evil seed begins to breed
when fed by naive folk,
it can grow with rapid speed,
the outcome is no joke.

And rising from the ash of hate,
can gain control of power,
democracy cannot dictate
when madmen's hearts are sour.

The fear begins to infiltrate
no one can stop the rot,
a monster born will not abate,
until the people stop.

Beware: manipulation stings,
the people can be duped,
be sure to follow goodly things,
as evil can regroup.

In Germany 1930s poverty gripped a Nation and they were looking for a strong leader to take control. Slowly Hitler gained a following, albeit small at first, until the rolling ball gathered momentum and he took control. The people were manipulated in much the same way that the British people were manipulated into voting to leave Europe. The naivety of a Nation can change the course of history and are then left with much regret.

The Rook

He's black as coal, he loves to run,
but he will fly, if close you come.
For worms his long beak digs a hole,
he loves to run, he's black as coal.

He makes a sound, a kaah a click,
this stoic bird is very quick.
This marquis of the tower abound
a kaah, a click, he makes a sound.

For shaggy trousers, he is famed,
he wears them out on my terrain,
when he hides among the flowers,
he is famed for shaggy trousers.

"Dolly's Poetry Pudding"

The Salon

Those scissors lurk and jerk so quick,
and final are the blades;
and nimble hands at work so slick,
hair falls in great cascades.

A tear appears upon my cheek,
those scissors near my ears,
they squeak and click and seem to speak
they fill my heart with tears.

My stylist kindly recommends
new styles to cheer my mood.
Short hair will pay you dividends
she makes me feel renewed.

Combing, blowing, brushing, spraying
my style is almost done.
Now it's time for all my praying
that's when I'm overcome!

I take a glance, the shock hits hard,
I brush away my tear.
The girl, she took me off my guard,
my curls have disappeared!

The Search is On!

We all know that love needs attraction,
and together we like interaction;
the search has begun,
to find only one,
who brings us that sweet satisfaction.

The Seasons

My path is strewn with leaves of old,
now turning brown with autumn gold;
yet birds still sing a song of cheer,
they have no fear of feeling cold.

But I suspect they plan to steer
and navigate a flight I hear,
to southern warmer sunny climes,
though some birds will still persevere.

The darker nights of winter times,
with frost and snow, all life confines,
will start to melt when there is spring,
each season has its own designs.

But Summer has a special ring,
for roses bloom and blackbirds sing,
and picnics are my favourite thing,
a smile is what the sun can bring.

"Christine Burrows"

The Secret Poet

As night descends I hear familiar sounds,
an engine roar, a barking dog, a clanging gate.
And soon when midnight comes the silence crowns,
my tapping keys, in lowly light, I stay up late.

It's then my muse starts dancing to my tune,
a story born, a vibrant bud will start to grow.
My window open, I can see the moon,
the town's asleep, and time is slow, ideas flow.

My poem moves from mind to brand new page,
arranged in verse, inclined to rhyme, with loving words.
I released like stars they're on the stage,
now my concerns will enter hearts of connoisseurs.

"Dolly's Poetry Pudding"

The Sparkle Returns

Tinsel town adorns
on white Christmas chilly nights
sparkling snowy storms

The Storm Would Spread

As stormy clouds collected overhead.
and anger filled the air with fearful doubt;
a gust of wind would blow, the rain would spread.

No one could stop the warring rage ahead,
its nostrils flared, its temper was devout,
as stormy clouds collected overhead.

The field was soaked in blood, the poppies red,
and silence fell before each one could shout,
a gust of wind would blow, the rain would spread

and mud would soak the trenches where the dead
had stiffened with an icy chilly bout,
as stormy clouds collected overhead;

as men were foolishly to death then led,
and would be shot if they tried to get out
a gust of wind would blow, and rain would spread.

The legacy of war where men lay dead,
confetti petals littered there throughout,
as stormy clouds collected overhead.
a gust of wind would blow, and rain would spread.

The Things We Used to Do

I know you wouldn't want us to be blue
so at the stars I gaze until the dawn,
remembering the things we used to do.

So many changes, means that all is new,
I see you in a photograph and mourn,
I know you wouldn't want us to be blue.

You have a grandson now, with your name too.
To heaven, he knows that you have been drawn,
remembering the things we used to do.

Your baby girl is fifteen, how she grew,
your heart strings pulled until they're truly torn,
I know you wouldn't want us to be blue.

But wait, you have two girls who are brand new,
so curious are they since they were born,
remembering the things we used to do.

The special thoughts of you I now renew.
To you my darling I am always sworn.
I know you wouldn't want us to be blue,
remembering the things we used to do.

"Christine Burrows"

The truth hurts

We know that telling lies is wrong,
that's what the bible says.
the truth should speak within our song,
it's honest words that praise.

But I have learned that honesty
not always gives results,
I spoke these truths, that recently
were taken as insults.

Now I've become selective here,
I hide the truth from friends,
arriving always with a cheer
I tell my lies . . . . pretend!

The Vapour Dragons

The electronic vapour puff
I see the stuff spew out!
The perfumed smoky dragon bluff
the snuff they like to flout.
An addict still cannot commit,
as nicotine they still permit,
a habit making them unfit,
too much of it about!

There is a cost

There is a cost in all we do,
all shops create a big long queue,
the time I'm spending standing here,
we could have been together dear.
As time ran out today, it flew,

and Christmas made its big debut,
the shopping trip too much to chew,
this season has no cheer this year,
there is a cost.

I do my best to persevere,
but I hate spending time in here;
there must be better things to do,
so much time wasted, this is true.
On-line I'll order all my gear,
there is a cost.

These Angel Wings

These Angel wings take to the sky
as birds have taught us how to fly,
and closer to the heavens be
to float upon a cloud so free
on manmade wings I'm passing by.

But leaving means I say goodbye,
and eyes are filled with tears I cry,
if only I could really free
these Angel wings.

The airbus takes me way up high,
to touch the stars I'll always try,
then down to earth to end this spree
as feet give way to gravity,
our final destiny denies
these Angel wings.

They took old Dolly down

All suited in blue gowns they were
and wheeled her on a trolley.
Fluorescent like the moon, the light
that shone on poor old Dolly.

The op meant she was wide awake
the instruments laid out.
They covered up her eyelids tight,
before they took it out.

Not one man spoke an English word,
she trusted foreign men
to operate, remove a lump
that never grew again.

So she can write this silly rhyme
and joke about the day,
those doctors took old Dolly down
but it turned out okay.

This Child of Mine

This child of mine just loves to sing,
because she has much joy to bring,
her innocence is worth pure gold,
her laughter fresh and always bold,
to her sweet words of wisdom cling.

Her smile is like a day in spring,
and when her dance is in full swing,
I take her in my arms and hold
this child of mine.

Now she has learned to spread her wing,
she cut the ties to apron's string,
on new adventures she enrolled,
and other people's hearts consoled,
yet every day I will still ring
this child of mine.

Three's a Crowd

A triangle is not so good
when under hood
descending cloud
three is a crowd.

And breaks a good and loving home
someone alone,
all left in tears,
remembered years.

The pieces then will never mend,
betrayal's end.
The marriage run
is now undone.

Tick Tock

When time decides to go too fast,
look to the past
and reminisce
of those we kissed and we now miss.

A stream of memories to keep,
we take a peek
and now alone
with thoughts of our long journey home.

Whilst there is life we live it well,
but we can tell,
time will dictate;
the clock ticks on and will not wait.

"Christine Burrows"

Time Has Grace

The time had given him some grace
they gave him a free parking space;
the hospital where dead men walk
where no one dared to speak or talk.

The waiting room was full of them,
they'd come to die once more again.
The faces with an empty stare,
the race was lost inside their prayer;

and no one dared to speak or talk,
the hospital where dead men walk,
as mean machines with laser beams,
internal organs washed and cleaned;

this silent room a pin could drop,
and you would hear the metal plop,
and hopefully a dream's restored,
but not before our screams have scored.

For many know they won't survive,
and some are barely still alive,
the hospital where dead men walk
where no one dared to speak or talk.

This poem is about the times I took my husband for his radio therapy to a special unit at the hospital. The place was deathly silent, no one spoke a word, people looked bewildered and broken, I'll never forget the atmosphere. Walking zombies, confused and in a world of their own dealing with their cancer.

Time Reflecting

We notice not the hand of time,
in youth we're busy in the climb,
our memories are made to last,
we seldom think of what has passed.
Until our future's short and sweet,
we are content,
we never vent,
and can't let go,
of what we know,
reflecting now is on repeat.

"Christine Burrows"

To Friendships

When friendships last until we're old
they're never cold with age,
because they are engraved with gold
and bold in their displays.
I raise my glass and take a sip,
and dedicate this little quip,
you're always there when down I trip
with your friendship rays.

To Pick a Flower?

Uproot or cut a growing stem,
a dying gem,
will not live long,
to sing its song.

As garden borders colour life
relieve our strife
sweet peonies
blow in the breeze.

Don't cut to please your windowsill,
and make it still
as living things,
need rooting springs.

"Christine Burrows"

Trees grow Leaves

Trees will s w a y inside a breezy day
as branches stretch up to the sky,
infused with life, I ask why
they are so green and gay.
Mother nature feeds
and always knows
s u n n y rays
will g r o w
leaves.

Illustration by: Faasai Slater

Troubling Critics

The critics love to stir their spoon,
release opinions all too soon,
to spoil our day . . .
and if a ranting rage ensues
as anger deafens when it's new,
they have their say.

But I believe there's room for light
as nothing's ever black and white,
when voices speak, we should hear
as listening could make things clear.

Not everyone can be in tune,
or understand another's gloom,
be patient, and cajole the flow,
not everybody knows you know.

Those critics who have much to say,
soon lose their bright and sunny ray,
when tables turn.
Imagine how words are received,
if it were you who were aggrieved
as words can burn.

A rose of beauty has a thorn,
so strip your words of bitter scorn,
in gardens let these flowers grow,
give those petals chance to show.

So let hearts rule, in your critiquing,
as your reviews may need some tweaking,
the help is much appreciated,
and everyone is compensated.

Turn the Page on Age

Old age can challenge, and become a trial,
and it will try to knock us off our feet,
embrace the future with a happy smile.

Our legs may seize, prevent the extra mile,
we spend too many minutes in our seat,
old age can challenge, and become a trial,

and woolly socks steal all our perfect style,
perm rollers in our hair are very neat,
embrace the future with a happy smile.

There's handles fitted to our domicile!
The bath, the bed, the walls of our retreat,
old age can challenge, and become a trial.

No work to do, and life is versatile,
in old age we don't have to be discreet!
Embrace the future with a happy smile.

Each morning waking up to life's a treat,
another day we won't admit defeat,
Old age can challenge, and become a trial,
embrace the future with a happy smile.

Uncle Scrooge

Now Ebenezer had a dream one night,
four fearful apparitions came to call.
The first one, Jacob Marley gave a fright
when dragging chains and ledgers 'cross the hall.

The second, Christmas past, began to haunt
the fun of yesterday, now dead and gone,
at one a.m. another ghost was caught,
no charity for Scrooge, his meanness won.

The ghost appearing last had chilling news
an early death became his fateful path,
and no one cared about this misers muse,
and at his death, so many people laughed.

The error of his ways was changed in time,
as Scrooge became a man we know is kind.

"Christine Burrows"

UNFAITHFUL

The twin girls were always so playful,
deciding to both be unfaithful.
They dated a man
not knowing their plan,
behaviour obscene and disgraceful.

"Dolly's Poetry Pudding"

WINSOME BUTTERFLY WINGS

Fluttering sepals
magical hovering grace
senses blush inside
quintessence personified
floating lacy paragon.

Illustration by: Evie Timmins

Waking Up My Muse

Today there's nothing on display,
my ink is dry and I could cry
as no more words come into play
oh why are they in short supply?

As inspiration left my mind
with empty head, I went to bed
I lie awake to try and find,
now fed-up, watch a film instead.

Then suddenly a rhyme intrudes,
and so my song, not lost for long,
I write as I am in the mood,
a stronger poem chugs along

My pen has come to life again,
and I infuse within my muse,
and write until I'm whole and then
I use my skill, for words to cruise.

Walking Into Disaster

When disaster is predicted
why are we not prepared?
If warnings are not heeded, then
we've earned what's been declared!

We make our bed and lie in it,
we had the chance to change,
why are we on this precipice,
we must all be deranged?

If falling in the pit of snakes,
we know we're gonna die!
So why don't we just walk away?
We know we all will cry!

The dye is cast, our fate is set
we're leaving the EU,
impossible, once set in stone
to afterwards undo!

We Thank you Ma'am

We thank you Ma'am you did your best,
as you stood up against the rest.
Negotiations not ideal,
the Europeans . . . made of steel,
your leadership put to the test.

Those in the cabinet protest,
resigned because they're unimpressed,
they didn't like the Brexit deal!
We thank you Ma'am.

United Kingdom is depressed,
and everybody very stressed;
I doubt reversal will appeal,
our nerves are now made out of steel
you did your best, and I digress . . .
we thank you Ma'am.

Welcome to the back Stabbers!

The house decided to avenge
a stabbing blade
would ply its trade
attack the back with great revenge.

She had to die,
you'd hear her cry . . .

The Politicians had no shame,
the race again
for number ten
another fool will take the blame.

Well Endowed

The young stud was very well hung,
his mattress was also well sprung,
as he took her bud,
he'd fallen in love,
his passion reached up to her lung!

What Lies Beneath

As oceans tend to hide what's underneath,
we often face the world outside with pride;
our tears of sorrow penetrate so deep.

As life repetitively brings relief
and what we really feel, we put aside,
as oceans tend to hide what's underneath.

Behind our eyes are tears of solemn grief,
alone we pray for peace, as we confide,
our tears of sorrow penetrate so deep.

A ray of light may comfort our belief
that troubled waters pass as they subside,
as oceans tend to hide what's underneath.

The path is often winding, sometimes steep,
but reaching for the stars won't be denied,
our tears of sorrow penetrate so deep.

Our hearts are touched by love, and it is brief,
manipulated by life's flowing tide,
as oceans tend to hide what's underneath,
our tears of sorrow penetrate so deep.

What Pigeons Like

What pigeons like to do is poo
they treat the streets just like a loo.
They own the town both day and night.
Their poo is often milky white,
watch out it may be aimed at you!

They also toilet on cars too,
you may complain, but they just coo,
from high on window sills they strike!
What pigeons like.

Some say there's luck in pigeon poo,
but if they dined on berries too . . .
your white sheets will be stained alright,
they love a summer pud delight,
offloading it, is what they do,
what pigeons like.

Winter Struggles

They struggle through the ice and snow to peep,
the yellow 'daffs' have sunshine in their heart,
with hope that winter soon is put to sleep;

and from the burrow rabbits chance to leap,
to find a tender twig or soft tree bark,
they struggle through the ice and snow to peep.

The robins scout for berries buried deep,
a frozen treat, this season, if they're smart,
with hope that winter soon is put to sleep.

As cats step out, but find the snow too steep,
and yearn to hunt and hide inside the dark,
they struggle through the ice and snow to peep.

And mankind warms its hands and warms its feet,
and leaves the snow to settle in the park,
with hope that winter soon is put to sleep.

The man now posting mail in weather bleak,
each house identified by its landmark,
they struggle through the ice and snow to peep,
with hope that winter soon is put to sleep.

Wishing on a Star

Just one eventful day can change your life,
the challenge means that you will sink or swim:
and hanging on to sanity brings strife.

The storm will rage inside your head within,
as long cold winter's nights consume your heart,
destroying all resolve, there is no win.

Dark shadows fall and tear your soul apart,
as grief begins to cancel sunny beams,
and clouds will fill tomorrow's weather chart.

When spring awakens pretty flow'ring teams,
no colour saturates your blackened thought.
As even when the blackbird's sings and preens,

a mind engrossed in gloom cannot be bought.
For time will wait for no man on this earth,
all good things pass us by if they're not sought.

The beaches kissed by sun still have great worth,
the trees grow tall with leaves in vibrant green,
and nothing stops our nature from rebirth.

There is so much to see in all these scenes,
release adherence to the sticky tar,
regenerate a heartfelt loving breeze . . .

Step back, allow you heart to stay ajar,
let hearts be free to wish upon a star.

Witch Hunt

A witch who had spoken in jest
got much of her angst off her chest,
but men of the crown,
decided she'd drown,
for she had no right to protest.

You are Not Alone

Do not feel all alone when trouble peeks,
as clouds disperse when seasons rearrange,
there's always someone else who also weeps.

Through history activity repeats,
no need to think a situation strange,
do not feel all alone when trouble peeks.

As hearts in love don't always bring us peace,
and death is sorrowful, engages change,
there's always someone else who also weeps.

And some will criticise with their critiques,
and there may be a heated harsh exchange,
do not feel all alone when trouble peeks.

If we can let our inner thoughts release,
a deep perspective serves to disengage.
There's always someone else who also weeps

in empathy, compassion will increase,
allowing us a break from our campaigns.
Do not feel all alone when trouble peeks;
there's always someone else who also weeps.

The Author's Biography

Christine was born in the Birmingham, in the United Kingdom, where she has spent most of her life. Her passion and love of poetry started at college when she was lucky enough to have her first poem published, 'The Beach,' at the age of seventeen. Since then she has developed her talent for rhyming words, and many more poems have been published on 'Amazon', 'Forward Poetry' and 'The United Press.' Her poems have also won contests on Fanstory.com.

Christine is also a keen chess player, and plays whenever there is an opportunity to improve her game. She originally worked as an aerobics fitness instructor for local authority gyms around Birmingham, and also Aston University, before retiring.

Her recent publications include a Children's fully illustrated colour poetry book, and a book of sonnets published on Amazon.com this year, 2019.

This is a collection of over 270 short rhyming poems on a variety of subjects that will make you laugh, cry and soothe your soul. A mix of poems to suit your every mood that may amuse, take you to brave new worlds, or even rock your foundations. Poems from the heart, filled with emotion or historical facts that chill us to the core. Whichever poem you choose, you will be moved.

The inspiration for her poetry comes from real life, emotions, people and places she has visited. Rhyming words are her passion. Her poetry is direct, and its message goes straight to the heart of a problem, emotion or truth. From wisdom to tyranny, love and sadness reign between the pages of her books. She also has a great sense of humour, and brings laughter into some of her words. Humour is a good way of breaking down barriers and reaching people's hearts.

Welcome to: "Dolly's Poetry Pudding"

"Christine Burrows"

Dolly's Poetry Pudding

A taste of something special is inside,
as words infuse with pride when they are mixed,
a guide to help you on life's bumpy ride,
a word or two, and problems can be fixed.

So take a slice of poetry with tea,
and I will guarantee you'll see the view.
The key to happiness, you must agree,
is being free to laugh the whole day through.

So keep this book to hand, pick out a treat,
not pudding, but a seat inside my mind,
a beat that's on repeat, a rhyme so neat
to open up an eye, unlock the blind.

For understanding how our life can spiral,
inside this book, there's art in our survival.

MMXIX

Printed in Poland
by Amazon Fulfillment
Poland Sp. z o.o., Wrocław